LEGION
RISING

SURVIVING COMBAT AND THE
SCARS IT LEFT BEHIND

JEFF MORRIS
WITH L.C. MICKLER

WILDBLUE
PRESS

WildBluePress.com

LEGION RISING published by:

WILDBLUE PRESS
P.O. Box 102440
Denver, Colorado 80250

Publisher Disclaimer: Any opinions, statements of fact or fiction, descriptions, dialogue, and citations found in this book were provided by the author, and are solely those of the author. The publisher makes no claim as to their veracity or accuracy, and assumes no liability for the content.

WILDBLUE PRESS is registered at the U.S. Patent and Trademark Offices.

ISBN 978-1-948239-35-6 Trade Paperback
ISBN 978-1-948239-34-9 eBook

Interior Formatting/Book Cover Design by Elijah Toten
www.totencreative.com

LEGION
RISING

For my mom, anything good I have ever done in my life is because of you and the example you set.

Anne, Cole, Will, Jack, and Claire, I love you.

Crissy, thank you.

To the men of 1/A/1-9 CAV and B/1-8 CAV "The Legion," the greatest honor and privilege of my life was serving by your side

Foreword

Young lieutenants have little room for error. Four years of rigorous education at West Point and a full year of intensive infantry training at Fort Benning do nothing to calm the nerves of a new platoon leader about to meet their commander for the first time. You want to do well. There's a lot of ambiguity and guessing leading up to that first moment. You can guess about the culture but can't know exactly what it's like until you're there. You wonder if the unit is going to be like one of those "horror stories" studied in the textbooks about "what *not* to do", or if it's going to be a unit memorialized in history for its performance. You ponder about the potential of the commander's personality and style, whether or not it will fit yours, whether you'll be able to adjust.

These were just some of the thoughts racing through my mind in the summer of 2006 as I walked into the Battalion Headquarters of 1st Battalion, 8th Cavalry Regiment to meet my commander for the first time. All that I knew is that I'd be taking a platoon to war, and that regardless of the circumstances, I was prepared to sacrifice everything to help the unit succeed. What I *didn't* know is that I was about to meet a person who knew the meaning of the word "sacrifice" all too well; a person who would shape, mentor, and guide me not only through one of the most difficult deployments in the history of the Iraq War, but also through the many emotional challenges in life that ensued for nearly a decade afterwards.

Jeff Morris emerged a true leader, but the greatest validation of this assessment can't be found on the streets of Baghdad. Nor can it be found within the countless acts of heroism he displayed, the impenetrable organizational culture that he cultivated, or the myriad of times he sacrificed himself for the benefit of the team. It can't be found in the operational mastery he possessed, his reassuring demeanor and unshakable confidence in the face of chaos, or in the number of times he "had our backs" behind closed doors. To be sure, the greatest testament of a leader's impact can't be fully experienced in the moment, but years later—decades later—judged only by the reputation he still maintains with the soldiers he once led. Jeff knows that leadership doesn't stop on the battlefield, and he makes a conscious choice to lead his tribe every day. He remains a powerful beacon of hope for the soldiers, family members, and community leaders who compose that tribe. You'll see this love transcend throughout the pages of this text, and it's perhaps the greatest teaching of war – when we lead through love, impossible situations start to become possible.

There are endless stories that I could share about Jeff's battlefield leadership, some of which I've already captured in *The Beauty of a Darker Soul*. He embodies the classical traits of the archetypal combat leaders who fill our Hollywood theaters and television screens, inspiring us to retain our belief in the power of the warrior spirit. But the qualities that distinguish the good leaders from the great don't often make it to the movie set. Leadership of this type isn't "sexy" or "flashy". It rests with the ability to maintain composure in the face of irresolvable moral dilemmas, or to hold a room filled with hundreds of teary-eyed Infantrymen after they lost yet another brother in arms. It is not about the ability to inspire a team to strap on their gear and "move towards the sound of the guns" in battle, but rather how well you're able to help them shed their armor afterwards; to cultivate vulnerability and give permission to process the inescapable emotional wounds left by those times. It's about allowing the souls that once lived to live through you, holding the space that maintains the integrity of the entire family. Jeff leads by example in this regard too. He is more of a leader today than he was even at the height of combat operations, and I consider it one of my deepest honors to be but a small part of his life, both then and now.

The lessons of this book have applicability far beyond the military. Where Jeff was a powerful source of hope for me, I'm confident that this work will also serve as a source of hope for you.

Major (Ret.) Josh Mantz

Author, *The Beauty of a Darker Soul*

Preface

At the risk of sounding overdramatic, the fog of war is a real thing. The events I describe here are my memories and mine alone. Most of these are events I was directly involved in, but several are recollections of me speaking with peers or listening over the radio as they unfolded. I have done my best to tell these stories to the best of my recollection and with the utmost respect to those involved. If there are any mistakes, they are mine and mine alone.

For over ten years, I have been encouraged by many to share my story and experiences, yet I always balked at the notion of doing so. The reason for this is my story is a direct reflection of so many men's stories and I feared I could never do so many the justice they deserved. To tell this story involves reliving the worst days of people's lives, especially the families of those involved. Despite this, I finally forged to courage to do so knowing the scars it may open for so many. For this, I am sorry. However, myself and the men also made a promise years ago. A promise to never forget and to carry on the legacy of our brothers. Everyone says this, but not all follow through with the promise. We have, and it is something I, and the men, take enormous pride in. This is not a book about me and the men, it is a promise kept.

—Jeff Morris

Prologue

Spring, 2007

Baghdad, Iraq

I refused to acknowledge myself in the mirror as I began washing the crimson smears of a dying man's blood from my arms and face. I moved methodically, as if it would clear the fog of shock that encompassed me. I tried to silence the sound of his agonizing screams that still echoed in my head.

A burning sensation on my face caused me to pause. I leaned closer to my reflection and saw a gash, running across my cheek, under my right eye. I stood still for a moment, trying to imagine what could have caused the cut.

And then I realized.

The skin on my face had been torn by fragments of another man's skull. Fragments that were embedded into the flesh of my own hands.

And in that instance, I stood frozen, feeling the image searing itself into my memory. My mind couldn't process the horror I felt, but I knew that I would never be the same again.

Chapter 1

"Boys do what they want to do, men do what they have to do."—*Steve Williams*

Destin, Florida

December 1998

As soon as the frigid water touched my ankles, I knew the next minutes were going to be very uncomfortable. During most of the year, a swim in the Gulf in beautiful Destin, Florida, would be the perfect way to spend a Saturday. The white sand beaches usually offer a stark comparison to the brilliant green-blue water of the Emerald Coast. But here now, in the dead of winter, the colorless sand barely contrasted the gray expanse ahead of me. The shoreline lay empty, void of the usual beach goers who were undoubtedly driven off by such a cold, bleak day.

I gritted my teeth and waded farther in, staring ahead at the horizon of flat gray water that extended until it touched the flat gray skies. A little shiver ran through my body, but hardly registered in my mind. The water enveloped me until my feet could barely touch the sand without submerging my mouth and nose. I drew a deep breath before plunging downward, the icy water slapping my face, and began to swim. A full mile lay ahead. Only two thoughts ran through my mind:

Why the hell am I doing this?

and

Don't quit.

So began this phase of my self-imposed training regimen, one I had followed for months prior and would pursue until the day came to take the Navy SEAL Fitness test. I was going to be a SEAL, there was no question in my mind. But I knew that following this path would push the bounds of my mental and physical toughness, and I aimed to be prepared. The dream consumed me.

I hadn't grown up in a military family. In fact, this dream in its earliest form began in high school as the credits of *The Silence of the Lambs* poured down the screen and I watched from my seat with one thought in my head: "I'm going to be in the FBI someday." When I enrolled at Samford University, a few paths led towards federal law enforcement: an accounting degree, a law degree, or service in the military. Something in my blood felt diametrically opposed to being an accountant, and I thought that a law degree would serve me well, so I chose to pursue law school. I studied hard and paid attention, and it seemed a good fit for me, even enjoyable. But even so, I found myself deeply drawn toward the history classes where we studied and discussed war, victory, defeat, and the great men who brought it all about. Thick history books weighed down my backpack, and I pored over the pages in my dorm. My interest in the military was like a kindled flame burning just under the surface, waiting to alter my life's course.

And it did. It happened the day I took the L-SAT. I had studied hard and by every indication was positioned to do well. But as I sat there at my desk, staring at the pages of the test, a restlessness overtook me. I blinked and stared harder, wrestling my focus back to the present. But an overwhelming feeling welled up in me, and with it emerged the urges that lay beneath the surface, ones I had tried to suppress. The pieces all suddenly connected in my mind... my captivated interest every time someone shared a personal experience from the military, the way something in me came to life when I watched a war movie, the deep pull I felt toward beefy history books and the autobiographies of great generals. There in the quiet of that testing room, on that cold, flat desk seat, I finally allowed myself to face the desire that had only burned stronger. Somehow, it was clear now that becoming a lawyer or an FBI agent would not satisfy me. I knew with certainty that day that I would join the military. I tried to finish the test to the best of my ability, but my heart and mind were far from those pages. When I received a less-than-ideal score on the test, it prompted neither surprise nor disappointment in me. And that's when I made a pact, along with a close friend of mine, that we would not only join the military, but we would become Navy SEALs. This dream became my one and only pursuit, and I wanted to immerse myself in it and push myself as far as possible. I wanted to chase the greatest challenge I could find, and becoming a Navy SEAL promised to deliver that.

When I filled out my application, I didn't check any of the boxes except for the ones beside Navy SEALs. I had heard all about BUD/S: Basic Underwater Demolition/ SEAL training, the six-month SEAL training course held at the Naval Special Warfare Training Center in Coronado, California. I heard all the horror of burning lungs, complete physical fatigue, and pain that came from the kind of training and tests that an individual must endure to become a SEAL. People told me stories of men coming out of the ocean, exhausted after a lengthy swim, and running through the thick sand that covered the beaches, and how those tiny, gritty grains slowly cut the soft skin of the inner thighs amidst the friction of running. But I wasn't going to allow these things to take me by surprise. Not if I could help it.

I would be prepared.

After swimming that cold, hard mile in the gulf on that wintry day, it took a minute to catch my breath. When I could stand, I jogged against the heavy water until I was back on the beach. Once there, I plunged my hands into the gritty sand and grabbed two fistfuls of it. I pulled open the waistband of my wet shorts and threw the sand in. Against my cold, wet skin it instantly coated my inner thighs and legs. Once it did, I took off running. I wanted to be prepared for the pain I would surely experience one day. The gray sky remained mercilessly dreary, and with each step forward the only sounds were my feet thudding against the earth, my rhythmic breathing, and the light brush of friction as my legs passed one another. With each print my feet left behind, the sand ate my skin raw. But I kept putting one foot in front of the other.

And I thought of my mom.

When most people hear that you grew up in Destin and went to Samford University, they get ideas about your upbringing. But my childhood was much different from any preconceived notions based on just those pieces of my life. My early memories took place in a tiny apartment, and by the time I was six years old, my parents had divorced. In many ways that was a good thing, as the majority of my memories of their time together are not ones I care to re-live. They left me strongly protective of my mom, even at a young age. In many ways, those memories were the match that struck inside of me… the beginning of my burning desire to protect and defend, to combat anything or anyone who would overpower or take advantage of those weaker than themselves.

After the divorce, my mom worked hard to make ends meet. My older brother and I came home by ourselves after school. He was eight and I was six. My mom was working as a bartender, which meant she didn't return home until late into the night. When dinnertime came, I might pull out a small skillet and dump raw ground beef in it, patting and tossing the meat until it looked brown. I'd open a can of spaghetti sauce and mix it with the beef as water began to boil for the pasta noodles. Even at six years old, I knew how to make meals for our little family. Everyone had to pitch in if we were going to make it, and I understood that. Sometimes it was a struggle. Even though I was the youngest, I learned to pick up on the signals—that look on Mom's face or the fact that we were eating canned SPAM at the dinner table again or living with no electricity until we could pay the bill. Whether or not the situation actually called for it, I believed that I had to be the man of the family and made it my mission to help my mom in every way possible.

Many nights she got home late from work and woke up her sons not long after. The three of us would dress and hurry to the car to deliver newspapers on the paper route she ran to make a little extra money. There in the dark backseat of the car, my brother and I would roll the newspapers and hand them to her as she threw them into the dewy yards, in front of the quiet houses where other mothers and children lay peacefully unaware and fast asleep in their beds. But we didn't complain. When you're a child, whatever your daily life holds seems completely normal to you. I learned through watching my mom what it meant to work hard, to never give up when things are tough. There must have been times when she looked at piling bills and felt overwhelmed. There must have been days when her alarm clock rang in the middle of the night, calling her to work when she ached to stay in her bed for just a few more hours. But she never gave up. Watching her taught me what resilience looks like, how to persevere when things get hard. And that would be a lesson I would carry with me when facing many challenging circumstances throughout my life. Even when I wanted to give up.

And that fueled me as I pushed ahead on that icy beach. Step after step. Breath after breath.

***

As a boy, I never wanted my performance in school to be one more thing my mom had to worry about, so I studied hard and made good grades. I saw how hard my mother worked and felt responsible for her. When she picked up odd jobs, I would rush to her side and try to help as best I could. My mom eventually remarried, making my baseball coach, Dennis, my stepfather. Dennis was ten years younger than my mom. At the age of twenty-two, he not only became a husband but also stepfather to two young boys. Dennis never tried to replace our father and he didn't inappropriately try to be our friend. He was simply there to be whatever we wanted or needed him to be. And we appreciated that. Dennis never shied away from hard work, either. He was a fireman, but always worked multiple other side jobs on his off days. He continued to coach our baseball teams and always sacrificed his own time for our family, showing me another example of a diligent work ethic as he demonstrated what it takes to be a man in this world.

Because he was older and could understand things on a much deeper level, the divorce had a greater impact on my brother as a child. He did not excel in school as I did and occasionally was the target of bullying. Whether or not he wanted me to, I made it my goal to protect him and stand up for him. It helped that as a young kid, and through middle school, I was tall for my age. If kids picked on my brother, I charged to his defense. I had no trouble putting myself right in the middle of an intense situation, if it meant sticking up for someone in need. Once, during a fight at the bus stop after school, one kid was easily getting the best of the other. He kept going after him even after the other kid had obviously conceded and laid curled up on the ground. As he moved in again, I stepped in and told him if he wanted to inflict any more punishment he would have to go through me first. Our eyes locked and he eventually backed down.

But for all that bravado and bravery, I never felt strong enough to stand up for myself. Running to the defense of someone else came without hesitation, backing up my position with whatever means were necessary. And yet when it came to personal matters, when no one was affected but me, I froze. Something soft and weak overtook me, making me feel powerless. I hated that part of myself. I remember being thirteen and proudly walking into school with a light gray and blue Billabong jacket my dad had given me. I didn't see my dad all that much, but we lived in the same town so we had some contact. He poured on the presents and treats when we were together, perhaps trying to make up for all that our relationship was missing at the time. And this jacket was one of my favorite gifts of all. Not long after I began wearing it to school, one of my bigger, more intimidating classmates stole it and kept it for himself. It was no secret who did it; he wore it every day, right in front of me, as if taunting me to do something about it. But I never did. I couldn't find the words to stand up for myself. And even more than hating the fact that my prized possession was stolen, I despised whatever it was inside of me that cowered in the face of a personally hard or uncomfortable situation. I saw it as weakness and detested it. I vowed to purge myself of that part of me. But as it turned out, it wasn't so much me who did the purging. It was a football coach.

Football was actually never really my thing. Baseball was, all the way from middle school into high school. I was lanky, thin, and fast, which serves you well on the baseball diamond. I showed a lot of promise in the sport and had the hope of getting drafted some day. But everyone I knew kept pushing me to try out for football since I was athletic and quick. Finally, in my junior year of high school, I decided to follow their advice. It was a gamble and far outside of my comfort zone. At that point in my life, I hadn't taken many risks. In my insecurity, I worried about being shown up as not having what it takes, or exposed as weak. So I went for things that were easily within my reach. When it came to the school dance, you would never find me asking out the girl that seemed out of my league. It was too likely she might turn me down. I went for the good friend who was sure to agree. And baseball was like that for me. It was safe, calculated. I was good at it and didn't have to worry about failing. That's why the decision in my junior year of high school to give football a try was such a significant one. I went out that spring.

And I hated it.

Every moment of it was even worse than my fears. And, with even greater passion, I hated my coach. From the moment I walked onto the field, Coach Steve Williams had it out for me. Coach Will would make fun of me and ride me without mercy. It seemed he was either flat out ignoring me, or he was yelling at me. I couldn't do anything right. Everything in me wanted to run off the field and quit. But I didn't want to give that jerk the satisfaction of pushing and humiliating me to the point that I gave up. Finally, the fire to stand up for myself rose within me. It wasn't loud or spectacular. It was quiet and internal, but it came with a deep, unbreakable determination to not only refuse to quit, but to succeed. So I worked and pushed and held on with everything in me. And he pushed right back.

Months later after preseason camp, Coach Will came over and draped an arm around me. He said, "I hope you know why I've been so hard on you. I saw something in you. Something good. I wanted to push you and see what you were made of. That's why I've been so tough on you. But you've earned your place and you've proven yourself. Things will be different from now on." And so it turned out that the coach I hated with such a passion became the single most influential role model of my young adult years. He took that boy and helped turn him into a man. He made me strong and resilient. I found a new confidence that I had never experienced before. And it began an insatiable hunger in me to see how far I could push myself.

I had once loathed Coach Will, but in time I grew to love and appreciate him. He pushed me to the point that I had to choose to stand my ground and not be shaken. Until trying out for football and being under his leadership, I had always taken the easy route, afraid that if I took a risk I might not be strong enough to see it through. But he taught me that sometimes the right choice isn't the easy one, it's the hard one. Many people will back down or shy away from that truth. Coach Will taught me to take action, even in the face of fear and my own inner voice that cried out for me to quit—if for no other reason than to not give the one I deemed my worst enemy the satisfaction of seeing me give up.

After playing well under Coach Will for that one season, several small schools began to approach me about college scholarships. Eventually, Samford University took notice and offered to let me walk on. Given that they had a pretty good lower level football program, I decided to jump on board. I would walk on the first year, and if I did well it offered the potential for a scholarship the next year. My dream at that point was still to go into federal law enforcement, and law school was my selected route to get there. Samford was the obvious choice given their high academic reputation and great law school.

With my newfound love for football, I couldn't wait to get started playing at Samford. But it was a miserable first year. They switched my position and I got my butt kicked daily. But after what I had been through with my high school coach, I was confident in my ability to stick it out when things got tough. After a hard first year, a new coaching staff came in, including one coach who had worked with Coach Will in the past. Funnily enough, his name was Coach Williams as well and he made the recommendation to move me back to defensive back, the position I was comfortable with and experienced in. Coach Williams did not coach defensive backs, Coach Mike O'Toole did and he became the next great influence in my life. After that redshirt year, I played on scholarship for the next four years, and our team did pretty well. My senior season, I tied the school record for most interceptions, most recovered fumbles, and took pride in my contributions. One day, a scout from the Indianapolis Colts walked up to introduce himself and said he was there to watch me play. My sense of success and accomplishment were directly correlated to a risk I had taken, followed by hard work and undying determination, which together gave me great confidence and fed the desire to push myself towards the next challenge.

And that was the point I began feeling the pull away from law school and towards the military. That hunger in me to take risks, and to see just how far I could push myself mentally and physically, growled with such a force that I became addicted to my attempts to satisfy its high demands. Eventually, the memorable day arrived when I sat trying to take the L-SAT, and once I had the guts to face the implications of my growing desire, I knew it would lead me to the military—and not just any military service. I realized that only becoming a Navy SEAL would satisfy my relentless need to stretch my limits. Becoming a SEAL would test my merits as a man like nothing else. And so I headed straight for it. I didn't need Coach Will to yell in my ears to push past what I thought I was capable of. That became an inner voice that whispered without ceasing.

And it whispered to me with every step as I ran on the beach that cold, gray day. For months leading up to this, it had been the inner monologue that nudged me out of bed and urged me to swim harder and run faster and rabidly train for what lay ahead. *Keep going. Don't quit. Push harder.* I stared straight at the horizon and pressed forward. *I'm doing the things no one else is doing,* I told myself. *I won't be afraid of the pain.* The chafing on my thighs from the self-imposed sand torture, to which I subjected myself on each of these lengthy beach jogs, sent pain through me like only raw flesh can. I finished the run without applause or reward, only the small comfort of being able to draw an entire lungful of oxygen. My breath evened out and I headed home, freezing as the warmth of my pumping blood diminished.

I'd be back again.

Once home, I slid off my damp shorts and willed myself not to wince at the open wounds I had created on my legs from the tiny shards of sand burrowing into my skin. I slathered Neosporin and salve over them and walked bowlegged to bed, a gait that experience had taught me would last for several days. Sure it hurt. But damn it, I'd be ready.

And I hoped to God that I was a few months later, as I drove towards Eglin Air Force Base, in the Florida panhandle, located near where I grew up. It was mid-February and testing day had come. Away from the beaches, situated somewhere in between Eglin Air Force Base and Hurlburt Air Force Base (home of the Air Force Special Operations Command), there was an intercoastal waterway that resembled a bay. That's where I would be taking the swimming portion of the test. In my eagerness, I arrived early and sat waiting at a park that was just across the street from Hurlburt. The day was bright and sunny, and warmth ran through my body as I sat waiting in my swim shorts. After training in the cold for so many months throughout the fall and winter, the warmth was a welcome change.

The buddy of mine who vowed with me to become a Navy SEAL had a father who was well connected and a Navy SEAL himself. He had helped to arrange my test and, as it turned out, the assessment would be one-on-one. There would be no hiding amongst a sea of other bodies beside me, no high fives or encouraging words from other nervous participants. No hiding it if I screwed up. Just me and him. I would be taking this test alone.

But being by myself didn't bother me. My brother and I had been taking care of ourselves since we were young. Being independent, going it alone—this was familiar territory. All through my formative years, I had fostered the belief that there's only one person in life that you can count on, yourself. If you want to make something happen, you have to make it happen on your own. Don't rely on other people. As I sat waiting for my test, a quote that I had read years ago came to mind. I do not remember who said it but it always resonated with me: *"We are all buried alone. We come into this world alone and we leave alone. Anything you want in life or want to be in life, you have to attain alone."* I had battled with these words as a child. I didn't want to be alone. I questioned why it had to be this way. I wondered what I had done to deserve this lonely path. But none of that mattered to me any more. I trained alone, I waited alone, and I would be tested alone.

Soon, a CJ-7 Jeep rumbled aggressively into the parking lot. The doors were off and everyone in the parking lot threw a glance the driver's way. There was no question. This was the guy. He casually strode out of the vehicle looking every bit the expected part, something like the SEAL instructor in the movie *G.I. Jane*, and headed straight toward me. He towered over six feet tall, sporting short brown shorts, a crisp black tee-shirt, and a hat. He even had a very respectable mustache, which only added to his larger-than-life persona.

"Hello, sir!" I managed.

"Call me Chief, Master Chief," he said. He introduced himself briefly and then said the words I'd been waiting for, "Let's get started." He walked me through everything that would be expected of me that day so I wouldn't have any confusion.

We walked to the bay to begin. The water was dark and murky, but I plunged in without reservation. Adrenaline kicked in and I don't remember much else until I waded out of the water knowing I had made excellent time on the swimming portion. We went immediately to the gym where I completed the pull-ups, push-ups, and sit-ups. After that, I changed into my pants and tactical boots and jogged out to a track to finish the final portion of the test, the running. I bolted forward and it felt amazing. The air whipped past and my feet glided across the track. It was smooth sailing until I had completed about a mile. Suddenly, fatigue swept through my body. My boots felt like they weighed a hundred pounds. By the time I finished the run, I knew it wasn't as fast as I had wanted it to be, but I was proud overall of my performance.

As I caught my breath, Master Chief walked over to me and let his tough demeanor drop slightly for a moment. "Alright, you've impressed me, son. Let's talk. What have you been doing to prepare for this test? It's obvious that you put some work into it to accomplish what you did today."

Finally, this was my moment to tell someone about my self-reliance and self-imposed training regimen. Someone who would appreciate it. I had a captive audience and was eager to share. "I've been training hard. All the time. I swam and ran all winter long. I heard that chafing was a big problem for some of the guys, so when I get out of the water I take handfuls of sand and put it inside my pants to prepare myself for—"

A hand shot out and a tall, flat palm stood in my line of vision, signaling me to stop. "You did what?"

"I, umm, well, I heard chafing was a big problem for some of the guys, so for months I've been putting sand in my shorts to chafe my legs in preparation." I waited for a nod of respect or at least a grin of appreciation.

He just looked at me without an ounce of emotion on his face. In a voice that was calm but serious, he simply said, "Son, that is the dumbest fuckin' thing I've ever heard. That's like practicing getting kicked in the nuts. It sucks every time. If it doesn't make sense, don't do it."

I felt like a deflated balloon. All that pain, all the nights of slathering Neosporin on raw flesh, all the walking bowlegged like I had just peed myself…had been for nothing? But then the silliness of it became clear to me. I imagined what an ignorant bystander must have thought, watching a serious-looking twenty-something-year-old man wade out of the ocean in the dead of winter and stop to pile sand inside his shorts. The stupidity of it must have been evident to everyone but me. I played his words back in my head: *If it doesn't make sense, don't do it.* Lesson learned. I felt silly, but I simply nodded and said, "Roger that, Master Chief."

I didn't want to end on that note, being forever known as the "sand in the shorts guy," so I pressed on with our conversation. This wasn't easy given the less-than-talkative nature of my tall, intimidating counterpart.

"Do you know who John Smith (not his real name) is?" I asked.

"Who doesn't know John Smith?" he replied evenly.

And then it seemed like an absurd question to ask. John was one of the first men hand picked to be a part of the elite and mysterious SEAL Team 6. He was well known for participating in some of the most covert, dangerous missions in history. So of course Master Chief knew who he was.

Nevertheless, I continued. "Well sir, John actually lives near my hometown. One day I had the opportunity to drive out to his house, and he took me walking for hours on his property and we had the chance to talk. He primarily talked to me about life, giving me some pretty awesome advice. I am just a twenty-two-year-old kid and he is a legend, so I listened hard. I asked him how he faced difficult situations, how he pulled through when things got tough. He told me that one of the first times he had the opportunity to call home during his SEAL training, he remembers telling his mom that he wasn't sure if he could do it. He didn't know if he was cut out for it. His mom simply said, 'Son, if all those other boys can do it, why can't you?' Somehow, sir, it reminded me of my own mom. So when things get tough, I remember that question and I ask myself, 'If other boys can do this, why can't I?' And that gives me the strength to pull through."

He didn't say a whole lot, but I could tell by his face that he had respect for what I had said. "Well, good luck," he told me. "I'm sure you'll do great if you get a shot at becoming a SEAL."

"Any words of advice?" I asked.

"Work your ass off, never quit." And with that, he climbed back into his Jeep and I never saw the man again.

But little did I know how those words would become the theme of the years that lay ahead of me.

Chapter 2

"Everything in life has a catalyst and a limiting factor. Which are you?"—Unknown

I opened my eyes and tried to scan the stark room around me, blinking away the thick fog of anesthesia. I lay back and took a look at my shoulder, unable to suppress a sigh. This was not how I had envisioned things going.

It had been just over a year since taking the Navy SEAL Fitness Test. During that time, I had eagerly awaited the call from my recruiter—the one that would allow me to take the first step into training to become the Navy SEAL I was surely destined to be. My recruiter had warned me that very few get chosen, that it's not as easy as one might think to obtain one of those coveted spots. But I wasn't daunted. Young and stubborn, I assumed that it would just work out in my favor. My hopes quickly fell with a phone call from my recruiter informing me I had not been chosen. As time passed, I considered other paths towards my military dream, such as enlisting in the Navy so that I would have a guaranteed shot at BUD/S. And then as even more time passed, I began to ponder enlisting in the Army or Marines and giving up the SEAL dream altogether.

Throughout those months following the Navy SEAL Fitness Test, a deep pain in my right shoulder bothered me, but I proceeded as if ignoring it long enough would eventually make it disappear. But it didn't. It got worse until it began affecting my day to day life and greatly limited my physical abilities. It became apparent that I needed surgery. I complied, in hopes that it would fix the problem once and for all. I didn't want something like that holding me back from my goals. But when the first surgery didn't work and I was scheduled for another one, I hesitantly called my recruiter, somehow hoping that this wouldn't change my chances of advancing my dreams. But as I lay in the hospital, blinking away the anesthesia from my second surgery, the words that the recruiter had spoken on the other end of that phone call rang in my head....

I'm sorry, but after a surgery like this, no one will take you. That's just the cold, hard reality of it.

During my recovery over the following months, I felt lost. Everything up until that point had all made sense; every choice I made was with a singular end goal in mind. And suddenly that was taken away from me. I took a financial consulting job, which was, at the very least, a step up from the movie theater position I held through high school and college. But it turned out that the only knack I had in financial consulting was driving myself further and further into debt. I hated to admit it, but I was struggling. The only bright spot during that time was meeting a girl named Crissy. She was half-Filipino, with a big smile and striking beauty, and I felt drawn to her. It wasn't long before I asked her out, and then it wasn't long before we were spending most of our free time with each other. As the fall and winter of 2000 hit, I finally came to grips with the reality that it was time to give up the military dream. No amount of pushing or wanting was going to resurrect it. I had a woman I was beginning to fall in love with, one I could see myself having a future with, and it was time to get serious about finding an alternative path and dream for my life.

I quit my financial consulting job and accepted a position at CarMax, in Dallas, Texas. Crissy made the move with me to

Dallas and it quickly proved to be the fresh start I needed, leading to a renewed sense of passion. My single focus became building a career that would support my dreams of family, and would ensure that any future children wouldn't have to face the same challenges that I did as a kid. I began my new job in January of 2001 and I completely immersed myself in the business, working incredibly long hours. It somehow helped to suppress the disappointment that I carried from laying down my military dream.

Following the move to Dallas, things began to go very well for me, and I flourished in the environment at CarMax. After a few months, I went for my review in front of the senior panel in hopes of becoming a buyer, which was the next big leap in my career path. This was a process I knew would take quite a long time, even if things went favorably with the panel. I did my best at the review and left feeling good, but still anxious. You don't get a lot of immediate feedback in those situations and I just hoped I'd get a call with good news for once. And I did get a call within just a few hours, from my boss.

"Where are you right now, Jeff?" he asked.

"Well, I'm at home with Crissy."

"Is it okay if Americo and I come to your house for a bit?" he asked. Americo was one of the senior buyers.

"Sure, of course." Inwardly, my heart sank with dread. Your boss doesn't just ask to come to your house. I was going to get fired for sure. The minutes dragged on while I waited for them to show up. When the doorbell rang, I was bracing for the worst. Instead, I found them holding a six-pack of beer in their hands.

"We've got good news," my boss said.

That night, they revealed that I was the first one in the company to ever be immediately promoted to buyer. A clear path was rolling out in front of me. The nagging urges and pulling in my soul toward the military seemed to finally die down and fade into the background.

But it wasn't a week later, while at a training event, that I struck up a conversation with a man I had never met, and my inward tides again began to change. As we chatted casually, I mentioned my dream to be in the military and how that hadn't panned out. He told me about a book he was reading, *Black Hawk Down,* and insisted that I had to read it. I bought the book and dove into its pages. Military and history books had long been my favorites, but in that year after the surgeries, I had purposely shut out every reminder of the military. From its first pages, that book was like a dry piece of kindling thrown on dying embers. The dream inside of me had been all but snuffed out, but was not extinguished. I read the book through the summer and couldn't shake the haunting feeling that being a part of the military was what I was meant for. Though everything around me indicated that I had found my life's calling, I knew I wasn't meant for it. My mind began to reel. Maybe, just maybe, the elapsed year since my shoulder injury would mean it was no longer an issue. I kept these stirrings quiet, not breathing a word of it to anyone, not even Crissy.

As I finished the last chapters of the book in late August, these thoughts felt impossible to suppress any longer. I strove to keep them in, but finally on one average Tuesday evening I had to tell Crissy. When I pulled into the driveway at home, my pulse was racing as I feared how she would react. She met me at the door with a hug, and I took her by the hand and led her to the living room.

"Can we talk?" I said. She only followed, clearly caught off guard, as this sort of request was rare for me. Crissy sat on the couch and shifted to face me, waiting expectantly as I sat next to her and tried to gather my thoughts. There was no good way to say it, so I simply began by saying, "You're going to kill me."

No one likes a conversation that starts this way, and her eyes widened. But then I spilled it all, telling her of that constant, nagging feeling that I needed to enlist. I knew things were going well for us. I was on the fast track to growth in this company. I knew we were beginning to build a future together and that this would change everything. It didn't make sense. But yet I couldn't escape it—as I told her at the end of all that, "This is what I want for my life."

Throughout, Crissy listened and nodded along supportively. She came from a military family and understood the strong pull toward it. "I'm open to it," she said when I had finished. "Let's just take our time and think about it."

The following Tuesday was September 11th. That morning, I had just pulled into work at CarMax when a breaking report came over the radio of a plane crashing into the World Trade Center. Shaken, I walked inside and turned on the radio, only to hear about the collision of the second plane. As I listened in horror along with the rest of the world, learning of the unfathomable terror caused by what was now clearly an attack, it was not just more kindling thrown onto that inner fire of desire in me. It was a large dousing of gasoline. Within forty-eight hours, I met with a recruiter and enlisted in the Army. After hearing a fairly favorable response, I went through months of meetings with doctors to get them to sign off on my previously injured shoulder. I also had to meet with several allergists to prove that a fish allergy of mine was not life-threatening, something that became a major issue as I got further into the process of enlisting.

Finally, I took the oath and a date was set for me to ship out for Basic Training in October of 2002. After all I'd been through, I wasn't so stubbornly set on becoming a Navy SEAL; I just wanted to fight for my country, no matter what that meant. I kept quiet about my plans and continued to work at CarMax as I waited for Basic Training to begin, knowing what company policy was in these situations. The moment you said you were leaving, you were gone. I needed every bit of money I could get to square things away for Crissy before my departure, and we couldn't survive without income from those last few months of work. So I kept quiet. But a few months before leaving, I was called into the office of one of my superiors. He was beaming with more good news of another huge promotion for me. I was torn. The company had been good to me and I didn't want to leave them in a bad position by taking a promotion only to turn around and leave within a few months. I knew that I had to be honest about my intentions, even though I risked being let go months before I shipped out. So the next day, I sat down and told them of my plans, afraid of the consequences but confident in my decision to do what was right. After I finished talking, they asked me to leave the room and so I did, sweating bullets. When they called me back in they simply said, "We're always sorry to see someone leave our organization, but we can't think of a more noble thing for someone to leave for. You have a job here as long as you need until you're ready to go." With those words, a weight lifted off of my shoulders.

I finished out my time working with CarMax in September, then set aside a week to see friends and family before I started Basic Training. While visiting my parents in Florida, I accompanied my mom on a quick run to the grocery store. As we walked down the aisle, I looked up to see none other than John Smith. It's not often that you run into one of the original members of SEAL Team 6 while shopping for food. I hadn't seen him since the day he invited me out to his property. We fell into easy conversation, and I told him that I was starting Basic Training in just a few short days. John had become a very religious man, and upon hearing that I was joining the Army, he asked me, "Can I pray for you?"

"Of course," I said. "Thank you."

He took a small vial of oil that hung around his neck, dabbed some on his fingers, and wiped it across my forehead before bowing his head to pray. I bowed my head as well and closed my eyes, my heart stirring at this man's words on my behalf.

"Lord, I ask for protection for this man as he embarks upon this next chapter of his life and assumes the role of a warrior," John prayed. "Please guard him as he protects others who cannot protect themselves, taking a stand for those who cannot stand up for themselves. Thank you, Lord. Amen."

It was a powerful moment. A rush of excitement and determination pulsed through me as he spoke those words over me. I wasn't sure what the coming months and years had in store, but I stood tall that day, ready to face whatever lay ahead.

On October 1st, I began my nine weeks of Basic Training at Fort Jackson in South Carolina. I was excited to get started but quickly found myself feeling old at twenty-eight as I ran next to guys and girls who were ten years my junior. Despite my age, Basic Training wasn't quite the daunting challenge that I had hoped for in BUD/S years before. But my perspective had matured, and after so many setbacks, I was just thankful to be on the path to serving my country. The training was much of what I expected it to be: mean, intimidating drill sergeants who knew how to yell and yell loud; strict rules and regulations forced upon you at every waking moment; attempts to mentally break you down and build you back up. I more or less knew what to expect, so it didn't shake me like it did a few of the younger recruits. But that didn't stop me from jumping into it wholeheartedly. I wanted to be the very best I could be.

One of our drill sergeants pulled me into his office one day. He explained that they were short on drill sergeants and asked if I could help out since I was older and more or less had my act together. We established a kind of "you help me out, I'll help you out" policy. After that, it became a game for me (and another older guy the sergeant had chosen to help out in a leadership capacity) to pitch in and then receive a few favors for our extra time and effort, but without the other recruits having any knowledge of our arrangement. Among other things, he placed us in charge of the weekly phone call rotations. Each person was allowed five minutes on the phone. Period. It had to be timed, and the moment five minutes was up the drill sergeant would walk down the line, hanging up the phones. He gave us the duty of overseeing and enforcing it all and then told us that we could place our phone calls "after the men were gone," and he added a knowing wink. We got to talk as long as we liked.

Other times, he would tell us to take the night shift for cleaning and taking care of the barracks. We didn't ask questions and did just as he said. And then while working, we'd suddenly hear our names being shouted: "Morris! Cheney! Get your ass down here RIGHT NOW!" We'd grab our stuff and run to his office. He'd have a college football game running and let us sit and watch it with him. Once it was over, he'd tell us to do a few push-ups and throw water on our faces to make it look like he'd "smoked" us, a term we used for when a drill sergeant makes a recruit do push-ups, sit-ups, or doles out other forms of punishment. We'd run back up to our barracks, acting out of breath, and tell the men stories of how pissed off he was and what terrible punishments we'd endured.

Aside from these benefits, helping out was also an eye-opening experience. Many of my fellow recruits came from absolutely nothing and were inexperienced in the most basic life skills. I actually taught a handful of them how to write a check for the first time. They were receiving money and had no idea how to open a checking account, write a check, or balance a checkbook, so I put together a small class. It gave me perspective on the wide variety of backgrounds these men and women came from.

There were a lot of colorful characters as well, like the strange kid who bunked above me. One night we heard a noise and popped up to see what it was; well, we found him biting his toenails. I found that both strange and disturbing. Then there was the guy assigned to be my "battle buddy." We were barely a few days into training, and I had only just met him, when I was called in with him to the chaplain's office. There I sat in shock, listening to him explain that he was a pagan and believed in the pagan god Gita. He stated that Gita was all about peace and wouldn't participate in things he might be asked to do in a combat situation, which made him a conscientious objector. Inconveniently, he had found this "new religion" after he had already signed his papers. The chaplain turned and asked my opinion since I was his battle buddy, but I was as baffled as the chaplain. I simply said, "Sir, I literally just met this guy."

Then there were the weird and inappropriate types I met who were not quickly forgotten. Like the thin, nerdy-looking, but very likable guy who stood up in the middle of the barracks one day while the rest of us were complaining about being away from our girlfriends and said with great gusto, "I vow to each and every one of you that I will jack-off every single day of Basic Training!" From there it became a running joke as we checked in and tallied his "progress" over the next nine weeks. Shower times were extremely limited; we were all given a mere ten minutes upon awakening to make our beds, get dressed, and be ready to walk out the door, and every minute from then out was strictly scheduled. This left very little "opportunity" for him to make good on his promise. But somehow he did. We all became a fan club of sorts as we kept track each day and everyone celebrated this odd accomplishment at the end of training, when he achieved exactly what he promised.

Though the experiences and stories were often colorful, I came to realize that these were the kind of men and women that I would have the honor of leading as an officer someday. When people put on a uniform they don't cease to be who they are, in all their uniqueness and human oddity. They are people who work hard, people who are willing to risk their lives, people who love their country. But also people who have strange habits, long to see loved ones, make jokes, or simply miss having sex with their significant other. It gave me a window into the mind of the young soldier and I began to realize that becoming an officer wasn't about just knowing my stuff, it was also about understanding how to rally and appreciate the mixed bag of people I would be tasked with leading in difficult situations. I held tight to this greater viewpoint, feeling that somehow this understanding would help me become an effective leader someday.

Though training went smoothly, my heart felt weighed down by one thing. Crissy and I weren't doing so well. Things had been strained between us in the months leading up to my departure for Basic Training. When I left, something inside wondered if leaving was the easy way out, without having to work up the guts to say the things we didn't want to say to each other. I was worried about what the distance and separation would do to our relationship. But when I approached the halfway point in training, I found myself missing her terribly and wishing we were together. I wasn't the best at expressing my emotions, but somehow being away drove me to a more honest place, and I told her through letters and phone calls of my feelings and my longing for her in ways that I hadn't experienced in a long time. It sparked something fresh between us.

I graduated in December and had three weeks off before heading to Officer Candidate School. My first order of business was to place a ring on the finger of the girl I loved who was waiting for me back in Texas. My mom and stepdad drove up to see my graduation and then took me to pick out a ring. It definitely wasn't the pure gold or diamond-studded masterpiece I wished it was, but I bought it anyway and boarded a flight to see her as quickly as I could. I landed in Austin and waited with my bags beside the baggage claim for her to pick me up. She was late, and each minute seemed to stretch into an eternity as I sat there waiting with that ring in my pocket.

Then she came into view, walking across the concourse, and I started toward her as she broke out in a run to hug me. Before she reached me, I dropped to one knee right then and there beside the baggage claim and pulled the ring from my pocket. Her face lit up as she realized what was happening.

"Crissy," I said, "will you marry me?" It wasn't terribly eloquent, but it was honest and heartfelt, and I meant it with all I was.

"Yes," she said, pulling me up and wrapping her arms around me. "Yes!"

We were totally broke and had only a short time before I was scheduled to leave again for Officer Candidate School, so we decided to get married fast. We threw together as many arrangements as we could and were wed only nine days later. We had a small ceremony on the beach with a few friends and family, followed by a barbecue cookout at her parents' house. It wasn't extravagant or meticulously planned, but I was grateful to have a ring on her finger and a promise between us before I left again. We savored the few precious days that we had together as a married couple, knowing that with every passing hour I was closer to being gone once more.

Chapter 3

"I don't want to waste a failure"—Nick Saban

It was a cold New Year's Day when I kissed my wife of just one week goodbye. It was a bittersweet moment, standing on the front porch in the early morning quiet, the sun just beginning to crest the horizon. Excitement filled me for the journey to be embarked upon, and yet it was almost painful to leave my bride so soon. It was a new year, a time of change, one phase ending as another began. At last I squeezed her hand and walked to my car, and when I looked back she was still watching from the porch, still waving as I passed from view.

I drove to meet up with a group of guys who were all headed to Officer Candidate School (OCS). One of them offered to let us crash at his place that night so that we could drive out to Fort Benning together early the next morning. It was a perfect plan. We'd get a good night's sleep and show up fresh and prepared to take the physical test, which would be the first order of business. But that night, as luck would have it, we all got food poisoning from Chinese take-out. And we got it bad. Like the others, I spent the night crouching over a toilet in one position or another, feeling sicker than I had ever felt in my life. As I knelt on the bathroom floor, my head resting against the wall and my hands on the cold porcelain as my stomach clenched and heaved, this was all I could think: *This is not going to stop me from passing that test. And I am never eating Chinese food again.*

The next morning, we dragged ourselves to the car and made the drive to Fort Benning. On arrival, the very first thing we had to do was take the physical test, which consisted of max push-ups in two minutes, max sit-ups in two minutes, followed by a two-mile run. The minimum requirements would have been more than doable for all of us on a normal day, but after hours of watching our insides spill out from both ends, we were at far less than 100% capacity. But the military does not give you a pass just because you ate some bad Kung Pao chicken. The alternative to taking the test and passing it would bring a serious delay in our plans. So at 4:30 in the morning, we pressed through what will remain some of the most miserable minutes of our entire lives. But we pushed on, hoping to God that we passed the minimum requirements. We apologized to the unlucky drill sergeants who were tasked with conducting our test, due to the fact that a good many of us were doing sit-ups while simultaneously vomiting and soiling ourselves. But somehow we made it. We sure didn't set any records that day, but we were thrilled just to have barely eked by.

The following weeks were, in many ways, much like Basic Training. We were given a similar, highly regimented schedule. Every moment of the day was full of something. About half the men were like me, in that they had just come from Basic Training and were taking the next steps towards becoming an officer. The other half, however, were enlisted men who had a good bit of experience and had already seen their fair share of action. The guy I bunked with was one of the more experienced types, as well as the two guys who roomed right next to us, Matt Mousseau and Chunka Smith. As I made my way through OCS, they provided much insight on how the subjects we were learning would apply in real-life situations. They told me many stories, opening my eyes to how things *actually* went down in the real world. Though I learned a lot through my formal training,

Matt and Chunka were the ones who probably taught me the most through that process. They instilled in me what it meant to be a leader, how to rally a group and make them want to follow, and how to have a good time doing it. We quickly became close, talking constantly, and sharing some of the most gut-wrenching laughs I've ever had in my life during those months. Matt Mousseau, who was in the special forces (we affectionately dubbed him "Moose"), was especially instrumental in shaping me as a leader. He was the embodiment of the "special forces" type that I had idolized for so long. So when he went out of his way to communicate that he saw incredible amounts of potential in me, that he believed I had what it takes, that I could be great at this, it meant the world. In fact, in OCS everyone is called "Candidate"—you don't have a rank—so of course this is how everyone else referred to me. But not Moose. On many occasions, he called me "General," and he told me, "You're going to be a general someday." To say this was a definite confidence builder is an understatement.

I graduated from OCS on April 13th, 2003, and I was officially commissioned as an officer in the United States Army. I was branched as infantry, which meant that the next step for me was to go to Infantry Officer Basic Course. That didn't start for several weeks, so I had time to complete Airborne School between finishing OCS and beginning Infantry Officer Basic Course.

Airborne School was essentially what it sounds like, paratrooper training for the U.S. military. Widely known as "Jump School," it's conducted over three weeks. We spent the first two weeks learning skills like how to maintain the right position falling out of an airplane and how to hit the ground properly, and we did this by jumping off of ten-foot ledges and practicing a PLF: a parachute landing fall. Then in the third week, we jumped from a plane five times. Like most of the other guys, this was my first experience leaping out of an airplane.

Before the jump, it was incredibly loud in the plane, with the doors open, the wind rushing, and instructors yelling. Once you have your chute on, there's nothing you can do but sit and wait. So we crammed in a tight huddle for hours. When it's your turn, you stand up and move into position. Those who hesitate out of fear are grabbed and thrown out the door. The noise and chaotic buzz of activity creates a nervous excitement that builds as you await your turn. But then you jump. The chute pulls and everything slows down.

Suddenly you're surrounded by peaceful silence. There's nothing quite like that perspective, floating high above the ground. It brought with it a moment of clarity like none other. It seems that such an incredible experience would elicit high fives, laughter, or simply a moment of quiet awe once your feet touch the earth. Instead, I was greeted with the sight of about three hundred people pissing in a field. We hadn't been allowed to move for hours and it was the only thing any of us could think about the moment we landed.

Then it was on to Infantry Officer Basic Course (IOBC), which began in June in Columbus, Georgia. They divided all the men up based on the alphabetical order of everyone's first name. That landed me with all the M's, which was a lucky coincidence since it placed me in the same platoon as Moose. As they lined us up, we were assigned to be battle buddies with whoever was standing next to us. That placed me with a guy named Adam Malson. Though we had never met, we quickly hit it off.

IOBC was very different than Basic Training. Many of the men lived off-post and were able to spend the weekends with their family or spouse's family during training. The time I had already spent away from Crissy had been difficult on her, so I moved her to an apartment nearby. Since getting married, we had spent only a handful of weeks together, and this put pressure on our relationship. It's not easy on anyone to maintain a close relationship across the miles, particularly without having had the benefit of much time to establish a foundation as a married couple. We had barely gotten used to the idea of being husband and wife before I had to depart. Now, the difficult truth of what it meant to live this military lifestyle was sinking in, and it was especially hard for her. She lived near me for a while, but as summer hit, it became clear that I would have to spend most of my time out in the woods training and very little with her. She decided to move in with her parents in Florida and we promised to visit as often as we could. The stress and strain I felt between us worried me.

Moose had on-post housing with his wife and children and was more than welcoming during that time. Often times, we'd wake up and get our PT (physical training) out of the way and then head back to his house to shower while his wife graciously prepared us breakfast. We were very hungry by this point, ready to tuck into a steaming plate of eggs and a hot cup of coffee, although seeing Moose with his wife made me miss my own. On the weekends, most of the guys headed straight to the city to try to pick up girls. Columbus is known for having a slew of women who are hungry to marry an officer, so opportunities abounded. Given that my battle buddy, Adam, and I were both married, we didn't have any desire to go join the wild crowd at the bars on the weekends. Instead, we would pass the time together at my off-post housing. His wife was also in the military and was away training, and mine was in Florida, so we found camaraderie in each other during that time. We'd go watch movies, cook, or just hang out together during our time off. Our ritual became to trade off buying a bottle of Jack Daniel's and sharing it over the weekend. We formed many good memories during that time together as we'd slowly sip the bottle away and just relax in those precious hours of off-time we were given.

While training, we spent most of our time outside in the woods. Our nights were spent under the stars, which proved to be interesting. More often than not we'd just lay down on the ground, spread a poncho over ourselves, and call it a night. I was learning to catch needed sleep whenever and wherever I could, which would serve me well later. A soft mattress isn't always an option. There were countless storms in that area, which meant we endured many wet, rainy nights together, wishing we were next to our wives in warm beds. We often woke up damp and sore, muscles aching, but we were paying attention and each day taught something new. In those conditions, you learn useful things like how to effectively and efficiently poop outside, how to make a tent out of a poncho, and how to dig trenches around the spot where you plan to sleep so the rain doesn't seep in. As we progressed further into the sixteen weeks of training, the weather turned cold at night. To cope with the lower temperatures, we would often huddle together for warmth. At one point, Adam said to me, "You know, I think we're spooning each other more than we are our wives."

I couldn't help laughing - "I think you're right." We spent hours not only training together, but also laughing and poking fun at each other, sharing way too much information about our sex lives, and overall bonding like guys do.

Moose and Adam provided a perfect dichotomy of personalities and leadership styles, showing that two vastly unique men could equally embody a successful and effective leader. Moose wasn't necessarily what you'd expect from a special forces guy. He was short and stocky and the funniest SOB you'd ever meet. He instantly commanded a room and was often the ringleader of conversations that led to uncontrollable laughter. He was quick witted and instantly likable, but also knew how to turn the switch and be everything he needed to be when the moment called for it. He wasn't necessarily the best at anything, but he was great at everything. He didn't always have to play by the rules and was quick to improvise in smart, savvy ways when the situation demanded it. He knew how to make a plan, but was also willing to throw it out if it went to hell in a hand basket. He taught me how to improvise when the situation called for it, and we had fun doing it. Adam, on the other hand, was quiet and serious. His presence and disposition had something of a calming effect on me. He was good at everything. He was the best runner, the best at PT, and he scored the highest on all the tests. He graduated as an honor grad of his ranger class. If you caught him by himself, he was funny and talkative but didn't necessarily garner the attention of a large room when he walked through. Simultaneously watching and learning from Adam and Moose shaped me into a package that fell somewhere in between the disposition and style of the two of them. Together, they were the single greatest influence in grooming me towards becoming a leader. Through two very different approaches, they each taught me in their own way what *right* looks like.

During that time, I watched the news along with the rest of the world, wondering what part I would play in the war that was unfolding once my training was over. It was pretty much assumed that the action in Iraq and Afghanistan was dying down at this point, and we all speculated on what would be next. As of yet, the insurgency in Iraq hadn't really begun to spring up, so most of us were already focused on what we thought would follow. Little did we know how wrong we were. A few stories started to trickle through the news about the use of rough IED's (Improvised Explosive Devices) and the horrors they brought, but the coverage was still sparse enough that we didn't give it much thought.

I graduated from IOBC in September and was handed a date to ship off to Ranger School, scheduled in late October. I said my goodbyes to Adam and Moose, thankful I was given the opportunity to journey through IOBC beside them. While waiting for Ranger School to begin, I completed several other smaller training courses. Out of all the training courses, many contend that Ranger School is among the hardest and most challenging to complete. That inner hunger in me to push myself and test my limits had not been staved off by any of my training thus far, so I couldn't wait to see what Ranger School had to throw at me. But I also felt torn at the prospect of leaving Crissy again. Already my time away training had been almost more weight than our fragile, young marriage could withstand. The reality—that this was only a small taste of our lives during my deployment—sank in heavily with Crissy. As I left for Ranger School, she sent me away with, "I just don't know if I can keep doing this."

The first week of Ranger School was call RAP (Ranger Assessment Phase) week. Simply put, it's seven days of getting kicked in the nuts from every direction. There were fitness tests, swim tests, road mark tests, and land navigation tests. On the third night after my arrival, it was time for my land navigation test. It was pitch-black outside and we were given only a map and a compass. We had to locate a series of fixed objects, using the compass to keep us on track, counting a particular number of paces to find the predetermined location. We had a map with about nine locations listed on it, and we had to navigate to seven of them within the allotted amount of time in order to pass. For the knack that I seemed to possess directionally in all other areas of life, I had always struggled with land navigation. I was a drifter. And that worried me as I set off into the darkness to take the test, surrounded by the black, rising columns of the trees, the spreading branches overhead, and the moonless sky beyond. It was just me and the woods.

Often, the fixed object was nothing more than a stake in the ground, with a set of numbers written on it. Upon finding it, you had to write down the numbers to prove you'd been there. The locations of many of these fixed points were over a kilometer apart from one another. I was nervous and completely botched up getting to my first point, wasting precious time. I picked up speed as I combed the woods, breaking into a quick trot to make up for lost time. But as I stepped on a log in my path, a sharp pain shot through my knee as it twisted unnaturally. I grimaced and pulled away from the log, writhing in pain. It hurt like hell. Still I pressed forward, though with every step my knee throbbed.

C'mon, Jeff, I told myself. *You're the guy who threw sand in his shorts and jogged countless miles up and down the beach just a few years ago. You've got this.*

I may have grown up a little since then, but my stubborn tendencies were still soundly intact. But as my jog turned into a walk, and as my walk turned into a pained, staggering shuffle, it became clear that I would never finish the test in time…no matter how hard I tried. Dejected, I limped back to headquarters and explained what happened, which also meant taking a fail on the test. I comforted myself with the fact that I'd have the opportunity to retake it.

As the next few days of training continued, I coped with the immense pain in my leg as well as possible. The ranger instructors, who are typically known for being colossal hard-asses, were incredibly understanding and helpful as I tried to hang on as best I could, despite the agony from my leg. Fortunately, a two-mile buddy-run was the hardest thing I had to complete in the days directly following the injury. They even paired me with a guy who struggled with running so it made us the perfect match. He helped me press through and somehow we made it together. The instructors were encouraging as I completed each task with increasing amounts of pain. They continued to affirm the potential they saw in me and promised that if I could just pass land navigation by the end of the week I could pass RAP week and move onto the next phases. But my leg continued to hurt worse as more time passed, and I began to wonder, lying in my bunk at night as my leg continued to throb: *Am I dealing with more than just being hurt? Have I actually gotten injured?*

The opportunity came to take the land navigation test again and I pushed with everything in me. It was much easier this time to find each location, but the extra minutes required to painstakingly limp through the woods were adding up alarmingly. On my slow way through thick brush, headed to my third point, I began to think beyond this test and to the other tests that were right around the corner. We had a sixteen-mile road march scheduled for first thing the next morning, followed by countless other physical tests. Could I really continue, even if I passed RAP week? Was there any point to this?

A ranger instructor was roaming around as I gimped my way through the woods. No one talks or communicates during these types of tests, but he saw my struggle and approached me to see what was going on. I explained the nature of what I was dealing with. He nodded, "Son, you need to start thinking about exactly what's going to happen if you *do* pass. If you pass RAP week and this leg is really injured, we'll hold you in one of our med units and then you're stuck out here until you heal up. If you don't pass this land nav test, and therefore don't pass RAP week, we'll dismiss you and you can have the opportunity to come back and start again. So my question to you is this: do you want to pass and then be held in these shit barracks with the docs we have here, or do you want to fail and go home, heal up with your family, get good medical care, and come back and do this thing at a later time? That's the question you need to consider."

I hadn't thought about things quite like that. As he walked away, my mind turned. I hated the idea of failing at something. But I had that gut feeling inside that whatever was wrong with my leg was not going to go away quickly. I also thought of Crissy. Her final words: *I just don't know if I can keep doing this.* This opportunity to see her might be my last chance to save our young marriage. So I made the decision to fail. I hit another few points on the test and then waited out the rest of the time. As I sat under a tree as the minutes passed, the bark rough against my back and the sky black above me, disappointment at this failure pulled at my thoughts. But this was the best option available, I was certain. The dark woods were silent, and it was good to be still.

In the following days, I found out that I had torn my meniscus—fibrous cartilage that cushions the knee joint—and would have to undergo surgery. I would be lying to say I wasn't slightly relieved to have the validation of a serious medical diagnosis. However, that served as a very small alleviation to the intense frustration caused by the fact that Ranger School was the only thing I had ever failed at. In the months after my injury and being dismissed from the Ranger's course, I worked to try and patch things up with Crissy. We spent time together, had many long talks, and tried to better understand what each of us had been going through. As I healed, I also completed the Bradley Leader's Course, which didn't involve mandatory physical training that would have been detrimental to my recovery process. The course prepared me for assuming a vehicle commander position on a Bradley Fighting Vehicle, an armored troop transport with tracks like a tank and some serious firepower. In the next months and years I would become very, very familiar with them, and with their impressive capabilities.

As I began to see vast improvement in my injury after the surgery, I headed straight to the Ranger's headquarters to set a date to go back to Ranger School. It wasn't uncommon for someone to fail the first time, so they were accustomed to giving second chances. But I received word that my unit at Fort Hood had already received deployment orders and that meant that I didn't get my second chance to conquer Ranger School. Instead, I had to immediately report for duty and begin preparations for deployment. Though I knew from watching the news that the fight in the Middle East was heating up and I couldn't wait to be a part, it gnawed at me that Ranger School would remain in my mind as a personal failure. I knew that everyone in the military instinctively looks at the left shoulder upon making your acquaintance, to see if you earned the right to proudly wear the Ranger's patch as evidence of proving your worth through that rigorous training. The saying was, "You either have a patch or you have a story." And if you have a story, it better be a damn good one for why you didn't pass. Though I had a medical diagnosis and a surgery to back my own story, that failure only spurred my compulsion to find every possible opportunity to prove myself and show what I was made of. I promised myself that I wouldn't waste this failure.

As the days counted down to my date of departure, I helped move Crissy back to Austin, where she planned to stay while I was gone. We worked to stabilize our relationship, but a distance still lurked between us. I stared at the calendar with each passing day, knowing that all these months of training were finally leading up to what I had been waiting for…deployment. That began an irrevocable shift inside of me. I found myself withdrawing more and more, and not just from Crissy, but from friends and family as well. In order to fully prepare for what I was about to face, it felt necessary to pull within. If I indulged too far into emotional intimacy, it could create a longing toward home that would prove distracting in the coming months. I had a job to do and couldn't allow distractions to set in. One night over dinner,

Crissy commented on the shift in me, on how distant I was even now.

"Even when you're home," she said, "you're not *really* home."

"I'm not trying to be that way," I told her. "I'm not pushing you away on purpose."

It was true, though that did not help matters much. For there was no escaping the reality that the closer I drew towards boarding the plane to Iraq, the more I watched the news and began to hear of the uprising and insurgency we'd be facing, the more I withdrew internally to prepare for those moments that would undoubtedly ask more of me than any other situation I had ever encountered.

As my departure date grew ever closer, Crissy also commented on several behaviors she found odd that I had developed. I looked at pictures of dead bodies to prepare myself for things I might see. I found myself drawn to bagpipes and often sat quietly listening to their music in the time leading up to my deployment. Those mournful melodies pulled deep at me in a way I couldn't fully explain, and from that sobering sadness arose a quiet strength and single-focused determination.

When the big day finally arrived, I said goodbye to Crissy with a heavy but determined heart and boarded a commercial plane. We flew all night and through the next day, giving plenty of time to think, to consider how the different pathways and choices of my life had led me here. Sitting in my seat on the airliner, I watched the land underneath us give way to the dark, unending expanse of ocean as we crossed the vast Atlantic. We ate our meals on the plane, my appetite light, and I tried to distract myself by reading or listening to music or simply staring out the window at the unchanging waves below. Then we were over land again, far below, and we flew on until at last we landed in Kuwait, the wheels touching down on the runway with a soft shudder that signified the start of a new chapter.

Once there, we stayed in tents, waiting. It was hot and dry, as we had expected. We spent several days working out, watching movies, just passing the time, and awaiting our orders to make the final flight to Iraq. There was a strange lull that we found ourselves in, something like the calm before the storm. We finally received our orders and boarded a military plane for our short flight to Baghdad. A gentleman came over to warn us about the landing, which would be quite different from our easy touch-down in Kuwait.

"We won't be coasting to the ground when it comes time to land," he said. "There's too much

risk of shoulder-fired rockets and other threats. The plane will take a nosedive and pretty much corkscrew to the surface. So you may want to hang on."

An air of seriousness fell over the men as the flight took off toward Baghdad. Some shared what they had heard about the descent, which was apparently notorious for making your heart pound and your stomach lurch. It was a short flight and in just under an hour we were making our descent. I braced myself and my heart thudded as we plummeted towards the surface, cork-screwing to avoid any incoming fire. I willed myself not to lose the contents of my stomach like so many others had. At last, we touched safely down.

As we came to a stop, a surreal feeling enveloped me. The ramp dropped slowly at the back of the plane, and the warm Iraqi air drifted in. This was it. I stood up with the rest of the men, heavy with gear, and walked towards the ramp, ready to plant my boot in the sand and do what I had set out to do so long ago. As I walked from my seat toward the night's sky in the distance, each moment from the past nine years flashed through my mind: sitting at my desk while taking the L-SAT and knowing I was meant for something else, the long runs on the beaches, resigning my job and stepping back from a promising career, training for months on end, sleeping under a poncho in the pouring rain with Adam and Moose beside me, saying goodbye to my wife and family. Every moment led me to this point. Every situation, every failure, and every setback had prepared me for whatever lay beyond this ramp. I took my first step onto Iraqi soil, only one thought now on my mind.

Here we go....

Chapter 4

"There's no background music playing in war."
—*Travis Atterberry*

August 12th, 2004

The deep, throaty roar of the Bradley rumbled beneath me. I clutched my rifle, standing tall under the hot Iraqi sun. From the waist down, I was engulfed in the strong frame of the Bradley Fighting Vehicle that lurched slowly down the road, while my top half stood exposed. My eyes darted this way and that, assessing my surroundings. Sweat dripped down my forehead.

There were a lot of locals out that day, gathering in small groups at the edges of Haifa Street, milling about and selling goods just as they always did. But as we approached, the crowds began to dissipate, scattering like frightened sheep in a pasture. There was something in the air, some premonition that it seemed everyone felt but us as we moved forward. It was unsettling, watching the townspeople flock out of sight.

Like an ominous sign, thick black smoke rose in the distance, from the direction of the road we intended to take. As we approached, we spotted a pile of burning black tires and smelled the heavy stench of smoldering rubber. It was obvious that someone wanted to force us to make a turn in the road. But with every passing second, I wasn't sure I wanted to find out what was going to greet us if we did.

Unable to continue down the road through the smoke, we turned. A sudden eerie quiet fell over the entire area. It was the most ghostly silence I've ever experienced, and greatly unnerving. The thick smoke from the burning tires still billowed forth. I glanced over the other three men who stood in the Bradley, exposed from the waist up just as I was, perched and waiting in the front-row seat we had to whatever the hell was going on.

The Bradley Fighting Vehicle, to a casual civilian eye, resembles a sand-colored tank with the same tracks and mounted cannon that one might expect. They are designed to transport infantry or scouts while providing armor protection, with enough firepower to engage and suppress enemy troops or other armored vehicles, such as its 25mm cannon. A ramp opens in the rear for troops to dismount.

The first Bradley in our little band of three veered first and we followed its lead. Just as we began to straighten out from the turn, the blurry forms of several running men shot into my view. The imposing figures were clad in all black dress, their faces and heads completely covered. The sound of gunshots shattered the quiet. My adrenaline skyrocketed, pumping through my veins, while my chest pounded like a sledgehammer. With wide eyes, I scanned the area. A cluster of two or three men fired additional shots. Another two-man team followed suit, this time firing an RPG right at us. Fortunately it missed, going right between my vehicle and the one behind me. I heard a few more shots ring out from our men as they returned fire, causing our opponents to duck quickly out of view. I clutched my rifle but didn't fire, the speed of it all causing the scene to blur past. Our driver charged the Bradley forward, trying to place as much distance as possible between us and the immediate threat we had just been barraged with.

And then, just like that, it was over.

My heart still thudded rapidly as I tried to take in what had just happened. My combat virginity had just been lost in a matter of seconds. And I was scared shitless. All the training in the world can't fully prepare you for what it feels like to see guns firing at you, to experience the nearness of an RPG, and to witness the hatred and power of an opposing human force who wants nothing more than to see your blood spilled on the street.

"Is everyone okay? Anyone hit?" someone yelled. Everyone confirmed that they were alright and we headed back toward base. As we neared the base, an edge of excitement set in as our adrenaline remained high. Several guys had earned bragging rights due to having the chance to fire their weapons at the enemy, and we had a little fun spreading the news once we got back. But all the guys admitted to feeling just about how I did in the moment... plain scared shitless.

As the adrenaline subsided, a wave of physical exhaustion took its place. As we finished our day's work and then settled in to rest, my body felt tired, but my mind turned over the events of the afternoon. I relived the scene over and over and wondered if I could have or should have done anything differently. It had all happened so fast. Should I have returned fire? Did I react quickly enough? As I turned the afternoon's events over in my mind, a subtle craving crept into my subconscious. I *wanted* it to happen again. I wanted to experience that rush again. Next time I would be quicker. Next time I would show what I was made of. Next time I would jump into the fight.

***

It had been several months since I arrived in Baghdad in May. My first memory after landing at Baghdad International

Airport was being placed on a truck and shipped to brigade headquarters. The truck arrived at a large palace, belonging to one of Saddam Hussein's children, which stood right in the middle of the international zone. I was dropped off, along with a new acquaintance of mine (one that I had made during the waiting period in Kuwait), and we were told to wait out front. They promised that someone would come and get us in two hours or so. So we sat out in front of the palace, waiting and dipping snuff like everyone did when there was time to pass. Within a couple of hours, a vehicle came rattling up and several men got out. Two of the men came and introduced themselves as Staff Sergeant Christopher Walker and Staff Sergeant Armando Salazar. They looked every bit the part of the older, weathered, grizzly staff sergeants that you might expect. Sergeant Walker was quiet, polite, and respectful, calling us 'gentlemen' and 'sir.' After introducing himself, Sergeant Walker left to attend to other matters, leaving us with Armando Salazar. And once he began talking, he didn't come up for air for quite some time. I remember thinking that I had never met someone who talked quite as much as he did, but I was thankful to make such a friendly acquaintance in such an unfamiliar place.

Soon after, I was assigned to the 1-9 CAV, which was a mechanized infantry unit and equipped with Bradley Fighting Vehicles. 1-9 CAV was made up of Alpha Company (A/1-9 CAV), Bravo Company (B/1-9 CAV), and Charlie Company (C/1-9 CAV). It looked as though I'd be taking over a platoon in Charlie Company, which was stationed near Muthanna Airfield, in an area known as Karkh, so that's where we went.

Once I settled in, it was simply a waiting game as I anticipated the opportunity to take command of a platoon. It looked as though I would be replacing Platoon Leader Fred Saxton, who led the second platoon in Charlie Company. While waiting for the position to open up, my official job during those first weeks would be working nights in the S2 shop, which was part of the military intelligence area. The military wastes no time in putting you to work, so I wasted no time in throwing myself into my new job.

Two days after my arrival, I walked to the S2 shop to begin my shift, which started about 9:00 PM. As I neared the building, a buzz of activity arose from people heading through the doors, though it was normally quiet at this time of the evening. Inside, the S2 shop was a long, rectangular room with a conference table in the middle, some computer workstations, and a big wall of radios at the far end. This is where men were clustered. I approached and asked, "What's going on?"

One of the men glanced back at me. "It's Charlie Company 153rd," he said. This was one of two Charlie Companies stationed in that area, one being C/1-9 CAV and the other Charlie Company 153rd. "They're engaged in heavy fire."

This was the first time I had been directly aware of combat happening in real-time since arriving. I huddled with the group, waiting to hear the outcome. Word came pouring in over the radio of injuries and a possible KIA. Then after a few long minutes, the KIA was confirmed. It gave a surreal feeling, listening to the radio as the report of a man's death came in. It was so unlike watching a news bulletin scroll across the screen of a television back in the states. There I sat, breathing in the same hot Iraqi air that had just filled the lungs of a fellow soldier for the very last time. And though I didn't personally know the man who was killed, the nearness of it struck me.

Once the action died down, I returned to my post at the S2 shop, one of the computer workstations where I often prepared reports and did other work, sobered by the reality of the danger that now surrounded me at all times. It was a far cry from hanging out with Adam and Moose under our homemade poncho tents during training. This didn't even seem to be the same world that Crissy and I existed in back home. I looked out to see Platoon Leader Fred Saxton trudging in to fill out the mandatory debrief of the events that had just gone down. A heavy silence hung in the air, and blood covered his uniform. A thought hit me with great force: *His position is the one I'm projected to take over in the not-so-distant future.* I suddenly hoped that I was equipped to handle situations such as these that I would undoubtedly be faced with. No one said a word to him as he walked up, his face making it clear that he didn't want to talk. His crimson-stained uniform was a glaring sign that he had already been through a lot that night.

As I watched him walk in, I heard the voice of a man named Travis Atterberry ring out in my mind. Before I met Crissy, I had a long, close relationship with Travis's daughter, Kristin, all through college. Travis had been something of a mentor to me as long as I had known him, and he had tried very hard to convince me not to join the military, trying to convey the reality of actual combat. His words floated through my head as Fred came nearer. *"Jeff, there's no background music playing in war."* I quietly watched Fred walk up without a word, covered in the blood of another man, knowing that somewhere out there, a family's life was just changed forever. The truth of the statement settled with cold, hard finality... *There's no background music playing in war.*

My job at the S2 shop was not incredibly time consuming, mostly consisting of filling out reports, which I did by night, leaving me plenty of opportunity for other things during the day. Apart from my daily workout, I spent the majority of my time with C/1-9 CAV since it looked as though I would be replacing Fred Saxton as platoon leader. As often as possible, I went out with him and his men on patrol, trying to get to know them better and hoping to soak up as much experience as I could before being placed in command. I quickly fell into a routine that first month after arriving, working the night shift at the S2 shop, usually from 9:00 PM- 6:00 AM, catching a few hours of sleep, exercising, going on patrols in the afternoon, and then coming back and relaxing by watching a movie or playing Xbox with the guys until we were called to go out on another patrol or until I had to go to work again.

We were stationed in a terrible part of town, an area known as Karkh. Haifa Street ran right through Karkh, a large paved road with three or four lanes and a median down the middle. Urban buildings with anywhere from three to nine stories surrounded it. It actually appeared to be a nice downtown area. However, directly behind all of that lay some of the poorest parts of town. Shanties and shacks stood tightly clustered and mangled wires twisted together across a maze of tiny alleyways. A heavy stench emanated relentlessly through the hot air. It was a slum. You couldn't even drive through it. There was no doubt that we were in a bad area and that the danger was real. The men dubbed two of the streets near there "Purple Heart Lane" and "Grenade Alley", for reasons you can well imagine.

Just as I was beginning to settle into my routine, still awaiting the chance to experience my first bit of action and still anticipating the receipt of my official orders to take command of a platoon, another tragedy struck. On June 26, 2004, I planned to go out on patrol with the guys like I often did, but got caught working at the S2 shop and was unable to go, something that rarely happened. The guys took a Humvee out as usual. It was customary that once you arrived in the designated area, the driver would stay behind while the others dismounted and conducted the patrol. Jeremy Heines was the driver for Fred Saxton and stayed in the Humvee while the others got out. An RPG was fired at the Humvee that day, brutally killing Jeremy. When I caught word of it, the news hit me hard. He was the first man that

I had spent hours with while driving on patrol who was suddenly killed in action. I hadn't had the chance to develop an intimate friendship with him since most of my focus had been on Fred, soaking in all that I could while waiting to take over his position. But Jeremy and I had still spent many hours together, breathing the same air, laughing at the same jokes. And just like that, he was gone. That was the last time they allowed Humvees out on patrol on Haifa Street. After Jeremy's death, only fully armored vehicles like Bradleys or tanks were allowed to patrol that dangerous stretch.

Just a week later, I was called into the office at headquarters, anticipating the final news that I would be taking over second or third platoon for Charlie Company. But instead my assignment was to move down to the international zone to take over a platoon in Alpha Company. My orders were to pack up my stuff and immediately move to the international zone, to take over command. Disappointment hit me hard. I had spent a lot of time getting to know the guys in Charlie Company. Sure, there was a roughness to the living conditions where Charlie Company was stationed, but I preferred it. Alpha Company was in a much safer, slower area. Alpha Company also enjoyed much nicer accommodations and living facilities. I already knew how the guys in Charlie Company made fun of Alpha Company, which was fully equipped with a generous cafeteria, while Charlie Company had to make due with the weekly shipment of lunch meat for sandwiches as their only food. Charlie Company was right in the middle of the action and that's where I wanted to be. But I didn't have a choice. So I packed my things, said my goodbyes, and left.

I had about a week to transition and get to know the guys before taking over the first platoon in Alpha Company. As I walked up that first day, two unforgettable faces greeted me, belonging to Christopher Walker and Armando Salazar, the first two men I met after getting off the plane in Iraq. It was good to hear a couple of familiar voices, too, as Staff Sergeant Armando Salazar or "Sal" as we called him, picked right up where he had left off, talking up a storm.

After transitioning the previous leader out and me in, I was officially tasked with being an infantry platoon leader, beginning in the second week of July. I settled in without a hitch and quickly adapted to my new schedule. Things were a lot different in the international zone than they had been with Charlie Company. Our patrols consisted of taking a couple of Humvees and Bradleys and driving around for a while and then parking them at the university. After that we'd sit for awhile and maybe walk around a little bit. Literally nothing happened.

As the month of July drew to a close and August began, we started getting increasing reports of all the harassment that was taking place on Haifa Street and Talial Square. Word spread that our superiors wanted Alpha Company to come up and start helping out in that dangerous area. Up until then, I had been the new guy on the block in Alpha Company, learning from my men and settling in. But now the tables were turned since I had previously spent a lot of time with Charlie Company and was somewhat familiar with the dangerous territory where we would be heading. I passed on to my men as much as I knew and had learned from Fred and the other guys. We prepared as best we could, but I knew it was going to be quite a change in pace from what the men in Alpha Company were used to.

One of our first experiences as a platoon in this dangerous area was taking part in an operation dubbed "Haifa Street Smackdown." Charlie Company, the guys with the 153rd, and those of us with Alpha Company all gathered together and deployed a massive takeover of the downtown area around Haifa Street and Talial Square. Together, we took the fight to the enemy instead of waiting for it to come to us. Since Alpha Company had the least amount of combat experience, we were placed in an area in Talial Square that was fairly quiet. But we still felt the rush as we heard the sounds of gunshots and heard reports of the action going on all around us even though we weren't directly involved in the fight. Inwardly, I hoped something would happen, craving the chance to be a part of the action. We felt no fear, only excitement as you wait for your opening to get involved in the fight. After helping out that day, the guys at Charlie Company let us know that they would call on us again to help with big missions and such should the need arise.

Sure enough, just a few days later, we got word that we were going to start assisting Charlie Company in what they referred to as "Thunder Runs". That basically meant that we would help to drive a whole string of Bradleys up and down Haifa Street. We wouldn't necessarily exit our vehicles to go an official "patrol", instead we'd simply drive around the area as a show of force. We knew that they wouldn't attack a bunch of Bradleys driving down the street, so it was a calculated way to deal with the constant harassment that our men faced every time they went out on Haifa Street. Charlie Company conducted these from their nearby location at the airport and those of us from Alpha Company would drive up from the international zone to join them. And it was on one of these Thunder Runs when, on August 12th, I saw those burning black tires and experienced my first real combat situation.

After my initiation into the adrenaline-packed throes of combat, I began to crave experiencing it again. Things only continued to escalate on Haifa Street, and after we helped with a few Thunder Runs we were assigned to that area full time. As we did these constant shows of force, we were simultaneously trying to raise up the Iraqi National Guard (ING) to help take control in that area. They would often go on patrol along with us. A few days after my first run-in with real-life combat, we caught word while on one of these Thunder Runs that the ING was getting beat down pretty badly on one of the corners of Talial Square. We were called in to provide support and ordered to drive all the way up Haifa Street to make our presence known and hopefully squelch some of the uprising.

Making our way up Haifa Street, we saw something in the distance dangling across the road. As we neared it, the bloody, limp form of a dead ING soldier became visible, hung from barbed wire strung across the street. There's nothing like seeing the lifeless form of another human being flaunted like a billboard, inciting fear the moment the mind processes what the eyes have just seen. We had learned from experience that our enemy did this, not only to scare the locals and to foster fear in us, but also to provide a diversion from something else that they had planned. As soon as we saw the body, we all bristled with a fresh sense of alertness. There was no telling what was up ahead. As we drove on toward the southwest corner of Talial Square, my attention was drawn to a salt factory that stood there, its exterior piled high with massive bags of salt. This was the area that we had named "Grenade Alley" and I felt uneasy on approach.

Listening to the gut feeling that washed over me, I told my gunner, Scott Grant, to pay special attention to that area. I remained standing up in the Bradley, enclosed from the waist down, exposed from the waist up as usual. Almost immediately, a figure emerged from the salt factory, running and then firing a machine gun from behind one of the huge bags of salt. This was my chance to actually take part in the fight. All of a soldier's years of training lead up to that split second when he places a tense finger on the smooth curve of the trigger and fires toward the enemy. And that's just what I did. I fired several shots at the dark figure crouching beside the large bags of salt and my gunner popped off several rounds as well. The salt bags provided excellent cover, so we were unable to get a confirmed hit. But my pulse ran high and a clarity of mind overtook me as the action unfolded. When the gunfire died down, we drove toward the top of Haifa Street before receiving orders to turn around and occupy Talial Square and send a few dismounts to provide backup and support to the ING that was pinned down.

Once back at the square, I briefed my men on positioning so that we could place each one of our four Bradleys on every corner of the square. We individually established our fields of fire and went over exactly where the ING would be as well. As I briefed my platoon, a man suddenly came into view. He was running, but something didn't look right. His arms were placed awkwardly behind his back and remained out of view as he ran toward us. All of our attention diverted to the incoming figure as we tried to assess exactly who he was and whether he posed a threat to us. As he approached, we saw that his face was bruised and bloodied from a recent beating. His hands were tied behind him with barbed wire that dug deep into his flesh. His face was stricken with terror. He was screaming relentlessly as he headed straight for us, so I ordered my men to jump out and grab him, get him far away from the Bradleys, and make sure that he didn't have a bomb or anything attached to him. As my men approached, they yelled at him to open his shirt, but of course, given the merciless barbed wire binding his wrists, he couldn't. The men radioed back that they couldn't fully see under his clothes, but that he didn't appear to have a bomb or pose immediate danger to us. The man continued to shout and scream like a madman, clearly beyond reasoning with. We had to take control of him somehow or the situation could prove ugly if things took the wrong turn. One of my men drew out his sidearm and, with one sharp thud, pistol-whipped him into the relief of temporary unconsciousness so we could gain control of the situation. After he was knocked out, we placed him in the back of one of the Bradleys and continued with our mission, occupying Talial Square. We let out a number of dismounts in the area, while I remained in the vehicle and directed my platoon over the radio.

The sight of our band of Bradleys was enough to scare away the threat for the time being. The enemy dissipated after we made our presence known. We helped gather the ING's wounded and then we waited for a few other vehicles to show up to get their wounded evacuated, all while continuing to occupy each corner of Talial Square.

Then abruptly, from one of the rooftops, a grenade sailed down and exploded near one of our vehicles. From my standing position in the open hatch of the Bradley, I was in a position to gain a good view of that rooftop. I signaled my gunner toward its direction and we both tensely waited. A flash of movement, followed by the sound of the grenade detonating—this continued in an almost pattern-like fashion. We rapidly caught on and began attempting to anticipate his action with return fire at the precise second that he made himself vulnerable in order to throw the grenade in our direction. My gunner, Sergeant Grant, loaded the gun with a round of H.E. (high explosive) bullets that are designed to cause an explosion back, which was perfect for targeting people who are hiding behind strong structures.

Sergeant Grant fired and we saw what appeared to be a human figure flying backward on the rooftop. And with that, the grenades stopped. HQ confirmed that the target was down.(1) That was the first confirmed kill from my platoon.

We helped clean up the ING guys that were battered from the battles of the day and then returned to base. There was an unmistakable excitement that coursed through the air as

---

1. There were large balloons on all the bases that sit up high with a camera attached to them, called a JLENS, giving HQ a better look at exactly what had just happened.

we returned. We had been given a mission, and we executed it and we did it right. At the base, a reporter asked to do an interview with us, which we agreed to. I felt on top of the world. We had saved a few good men, the enemy had lost a man, and no one was hurt in the process. For me, it was a win all the way around. I had anxiously awaited the time when I would be called to step up and lead in the capacity I had trained for all this time, a chance to prove what I was made of, not just to the world, but to myself. And I felt that I did just that. I basked in the afterglow of victory.

A few hours later, I was called into the office of my superior and congratulated for a job well done. In the same breath, however, I was reprimanded for the fact that we had shot upwards at a building that was about a mile in front of Muthanna Airfield. It wasn't extremely likely, but in the event that we missed the shot could have landed right in the middle of the airfield. That possibility hadn't crossed my mind in the heat of the battle. It was a big lesson in situational awareness for me. I realized that you can't just think about what's going on immediately around you; you have to think of what is about to come and all the steps ahead. In attempting to do something really good that day, we could have done something really bad. With a heavy sense of responsibility, I came to grips with the fact that it was my job to think about all of those things. It was my duty to look ahead, have forethought, and direct my men accordingly. I was, after all, tasked with leading them.

My superior used it as an excellent learning opportunity for me. "Even through all the adrenaline, all the emotion, all the excitement, all the fear," he told me, "our job is to maintain a clarity of mind and think about not only the immediate danger we're faced with, but the greater picture all around." He paused, letting that sink in. "You've got to remember how important it is to take in your surroundings and account for the positions of both the enemy and your fellow soldiers.

Many times when men are harmed through friendly fire, it's the result of people not being where they are supposed to be. Or it's because soldiers don't take into account, or just forget, the location of the other men they're fighting alongside."

It was a valuable lesson. After we finished talking, I thanked him and left his office. With determination to learn from experience, I gathered my men and began what would be something of a ritual for us... to deeply embrace the process of the After Action Review (AAR) and assessing what went right and what went wrong, what could be improved, and how we could be better.

Though the weight of responsibility hung over me after that talk, I still felt good about the overall operations of my platoon in that situation. I received several encouraging words from others with decades of experience such as Staff Sergeant Walker, a man of few words, who simply said, "Sir, you did it right today." That meant the world.

The exhilaration of the entire experience that day left me on a high. Just a few days before, when I lost my combat virginity, I felt a shift take place inside, from feeling scared to embracing the rush of it all. But after this true immersion into combat, I felt excitement giving way to an obsession to experience it again. The rush I felt and the desire to feel it again was starting to consume me. As soldiers, that burning desire wasn't something we gave voice to or discussed with each other, but most of us felt it... that constant hunger to see action after our appetite was whet by those first combat experiences.

And those appetites were quickly fed, as we saw action almost constantly in the latter part of August and the beginning of September. It wasn't long before one of my men sustained an injury from taking a piece of shrapnel in the leg and received a Purple Heart. That tempered the attraction we all felt toward combat, but by no means squelched it. The fight in Iraq was really heating up and we were smack dab in the middle of it.

We all began to find our rhythm and to settle into our respective roles and responsibilities as our exposure to combat increased. Our senses sharpened and our responses became quicker and quicker as we faced continual threat and endangerment every time we went out. Fear still rose up when danger appeared, having lurked in that primal, self-preserving part of our human hearts, but the shaky anxiety that we had all suffered the first few times we faced tough situations gave way to a clarity and presence of mind as we gained experience. Engaging the enemy, which had been the exception, was now the norm. And we were all beginning to adapt to that truth.

In those months, when I was finally given the opportunity to lay my head down at night, complete exhaustion overtook me. The sudden absence of adrenaline in the body creates a fast and abrupt collapse into a fatigue that gives way to deep, hard sleep. I had few thoughts in my mind in those last conscious moments besides the constant replay and analysis of the day and the thought of what I might face tomorrow.

But sometimes, when everything was quiet and still, when all the excitement died down, my mind would be drawn back to a phone call from home I received in August, the very same day I saw those burning tires and experienced my first brief moments of action. Ever since then, I had been trying my best to suppress the memory of that call, to push it far from my mind. But every now and then when I was just too tired to push anything, even my own thoughts from my head, the conversation would come floating back to me. I would remember going into that little phone room right before going out on patrol, just three feet squared, and hearing Crissy on the other end of the line. And then I would recall her telling me that our marriage was over and that she was moving on. And momentarily, I'd feel the heartbreak, anger, and shame that had struck me in the moment when I had taken in the news weeks before. Heartbreak that my marriage was over and that a divorce awaited me upon arriving home. Anger for what I couldn't control. Shame from feeling that I couldn't be the man she needed or wanted me to be. But then I'd remember the icy resolve that had taken hold inside of me that day when I hung up the phone... to push this out of my mind, to refuse to let it affect me, even in the slightest. I vowed to myself in that cramped telephone room that all the wild emotion I felt in that moment had to stay behind, it could not be carried with me. And every time thoughts of that conversation came floating back, I willed them to return to that tiny phone room where they belonged.

I had a job to do. And no time for thoughts of anything but the mission ahead.

Chapter 5

"The truths are contradictory. It can be argued, for instance, that war is grotesque. But in truth war is also beauty. For all its horror, you can't help but gape at the awful majesty of combat. You stare out at tracer rounds unwinding through the dark like brilliant red ribbons. You crouch in ambush as a cool, impassive moon rises over the nighttime paddies. You admire the fluid symmetries of troops on the move, the harmonies of sound and shape and proportion, the great sheets of metal-fire streaming down from a gunship, the illumination rounds, the white phosphorous, the purply black glow of napalm, the rocket's red glare. It's not pretty, exactly. It's astonishing. It fills the eye. It commands you. You hate it, yes, but your eyes do not. Like a killer forest fire, like cancer under a microscope, any battle or bombing raid or artillery barrage has the aesthetic purity of absolute moral indifference—a powerful, implacable beauty—and a true war story will tell the truth about this, though the truth is ugly."—Tim O'Brien

September 2004

The sun beat down hard on my back and sweat beaded across my face as I walked up a small alley. It was early September and the hot, heavy Iraqi air pressed down on me, more oppressive than the weighty gear I carried. The alley was no more than four feet wide, right in the midst of the shanty town that stood in all of its shambled glory not far from Haifa street. Thick, raw sewage ran beside the alley—muddy water mixed with human and animal urine and waste—on its way to drain into the Tigris River. Unsanitary trash piles, left unattended, stood high in pockets around the area, adding to the relentless, hideous symphony of smells. Not far from where we walked, an above-ground cemetery gave its contribution to the unsavory stench as well.

Our senses remained on high alert as we patrolled the small area. Things had been steadily heating up in the past few months and today a particular tension hung in the air. Through experience, we had become more strategic in our approach as we patrolled these dangerous zones. Rather than following the typical infantry techniques of moving in larger elements, which would mean occupying two alleys with nine men on each, we decided to head toward the maze of smaller alleys so we could occupy several at once, with three men on each one. This also made us less of a target. By being more spread out and less bunched up, the threat of someone throwing an explosive and then hopping over the fence for cover before we could retaliate was greatly diminished. In a narrow alley, the enemy was less likely to attack because we had eliminated the presence of a good escape route.

We walked up the tiny street a little farther and rounded a slight bend. Without warning, dirt and rock blasted into the air right in front of us as two grenades exploded close by. In that split second, as the adrenaline hit my body and my mind flew into overdrive, I spotted a small opening right off the alley that could provide some cover and dove headlong into the protection it offered. Two of my men had the same thought and crashed next to me just as the wave of soil and rock rained down on us. As debris pounded into me, I wondered if I had been hit by shrapnel, but realized it was just the sting of the dirt and stones launched by the grenade's impact.

The three of us crouched in the small cove just off the alley, breathing deeply and waiting to see if the explosion would be followed by another. It's a terrible waiting game. When silence reigned, we charged around the bend in the alley and chased after our opponent. We ran fast, but found nothing. They had already moved on. We quickly realized that they were most likely finding a vantage point to target our men that were positioned in the other alleys nearby, so we headed in that direction. As we approached, one of my men, a big, stout soldier named Tim Hulsey, burst into view. He was running at full speed in the direction of the Bradley. His legs were pumping with great force as he neared us, a look on his face that couldn't quite be described.

"Are you okay?" I yelled.

"SOMETHING BIT ME!" he shouted, holding onto his backside and not slowing down as he blurred past us. I realized that he had taken a large piece of shrapnel to his ass, and even in the heat of the moment I couldn't help being amused that he had the presence of mind to quote Forrest Gump in the midst of being injured in combat. We continued our pursuit but were unsuccessful in finding or retaliating against those who had thrown the grenades.

Events like this continued to occur constantly as we pushed into the early part of September.

Around that time, we had begun to catch word that large numbers of Al-Qaeda members were moving out of Fallujah, where things had gotten pretty bad. The Americans had all but announced that they would be cleaning out that area in the near future and so Al-Qaeda members wasted no time in getting out of there. Insurgents began pouring into the area near Haifa Street and set up Baghdad headquarters for Al-Qaeda. As more insurgents swarmed into the region, we began to see a significant increase in the constant harassment that we had become familiar with when we ventured out. The insurgents didn't necessarily execute the legwork of these constant attacks; they paid poor, local kids and teenagers to do it for them, some as young as nine or ten years old. They were masters at finding young, impoverished residents that had nothing going for them in life and recruiting them to carry out their dirty work such as throwing grenades or popping off a few rounds at the Americans.

We had to defend ourselves when fired upon, but we all struggled with the knowledge that we were fighting an enemy ruthless enough to involve children in the dirty deeds of war. While no one in my unit was faced with a situation where children were directly harmed by a choice on our part, we couldn't help but feel haunted by the thought that when we launched a grenade over a wall, a child could be on the other side.

We soon began to recognize another pattern. After we patrolled an area, and once the harassment had died down and we had left, the insurgents would come out and strut through the streets in hopes of intimidating the locals. Many of the locals were already gone, but the insurgents wanted to display their power for the ones who remained. They would walk down the street with their guns in the air, proudly toting their RPGs as a show of superiority, bragging that they had scared away the mighty Americans. We caught on to the little game and devised a strategy. We would swarm into an area with a ton of men and all at once occupy a particular vicinity, including several buildings, purposely creating confusion. After a while, we'd make an obvious show of us vacating the area, while leaving a small team of SEAL snipers behind. Sure enough, once it appeared that we were gone, the local insurgents would come out dancing and making a spectacle of the fact that they had "beat" the great Americans. The snipers were ready, strategically placed in vantage points that provided perfect positioning for picking off the enemy. With silencers on their guns, they accomplished numerous successful kills before the group would go running for cover.

This strategy proved to be effective, so we continued to use it for small, short missions. We also began making plans for a larger mission that would include putting SEALs in place for a longer stint of time. The mission was set for September 12th. We carefully ironed out the necessary details for getting the SEAL team in position and equipped to occupy one of the abandoned buildings near Talial Square for forty-eight hours.

It was still dark when we awoke and prepared to depart in the wee hours of the morning on September 12th. The sun's absence provided a small reprieve from the unceasing heat that we endured by day, but the night air was still thick and warm. Alpha Company was tasked with dropping the SEALs off at the designated location. Nine men from another platoon joined us as well and were in charge of providing constant security so that the SEALs could rotate in shifts. The SEAL team was made up of highly trained individuals, all excellent marksmen. One platoon from Alpha Company headed straight to Talial Square with orders to occupy it. Another platoon stayed in the back and provided security at a nearby intersection. Our platoon was in charge of transporting the SEALs all the way to the location and providing food and water for the two long days they had ahead of them.

After driving for a bit, we jerked to a stop in front of an abandoned building that stood seventeen stories high, just past Talial Square. This would be the SEALs' home for the next forty-eight hours. It was approximately 3:00 AM when we arrived at the location. When we entered, it looked much like the lobby inside of a hotel, complete with a desk for the bellman. We didn't say much to each other as we pulled on our heavy rucksacks and efficiently began carting food and water up to the top of the building. That meant plodding up seventeen flights of narrow stairways, weighed down with our gear and rations for the SEALs. The buildings were furnished nicely on the inside. Some of the former occupants had taken their belongings with them upon leaving, but many had left everything behind, which meant that a lot of the rooms were left untouched and fully furnished. When looking in, it would appear that someone had just stepped out to grab dinner rather than leaving everything and fleeing the area. It was a strange sight. Once the SEALs were in position and adequately stocked with food and water, we loaded into the Bradley to begin our drive back to base. Everything had clicked along like clockwork thus far and the mission appeared to be running smoothly.

But as we began to drive away, the sounds of detonating RPGs and heavy machine gun fire rang out, exploding around our vehicles. I tensed. The enemy never engaged at night, primarily because they were not equipped with night vision gear. Something was wrong. We drove away, intentionally returning to base rather than being drawn into a firefight, but we remained on high alert. Though we resided in the international zone, our superiors had staged us at FOB (Forward Operating Base) Headhunter, the airfield nearby, for the day. We were on QRF (Quick Reaction Force), rotating with a few other platoons on standby in case things turned ugly. No sooner had we arrived back at the airport than orders came for our platoon to stage by the gate of the airport and wait. We weren't sure of the exact situation, but it was obvious that shit was about to hit the fan and that the day would most likely end far more eventfully than it had begun.

We soon learned that a group of Al-Qaeda members had headed to the local mosque, which housed a large amount of weaponry, to shoot a propaganda video. The SEALs radioed in, reporting that a mob of forty to fifty men were walking down the street in a show of force, carrying RPGs and heavy weaponry. The rules of engagement were different for this mission and rather than having permission to engage two or more armed men, they were ordered to hold fire until faced with a group of five or more. But with this turn of events, there was a different dilemma entirely. The SEALs were far outnumbered and there would be significant risk if they began shooting, due to the fact that their location would be quickly discovered and they could be blocked in with no good means of escape. But orders to go ahead and engage came through, and they began to fire. And sure enough, it didn't take long for the enemy to figure out exactly where the shots were coming from. To make matters worse, on this particular day, it appeared that everyone wanted to join the fight—every local with a gun, it seemed, came out to participate. The SEALs were instantly outnumbered and in a no-win situation. We soon received orders to go and retrieve the SEALs as it became clear that the day's mission was shaping up to be anything but routine.

We followed the same general plan that we had used early that morning. Third platoon sped to occupy Talial Square, and our platoon, which was headed directly to the SEALs' location, was close behind. Second platoon brought up the rear and drove to another intersection to provide protection. As we neared the area, we were met with an extreme barrage of RPGs and gunfire. It was like nothing I had ever experienced. The fire came from every direction, surrounding us on all sides. My platoon was tasked with retrieving the SEALs, who were ready and waiting for us on the second floor of the building. Our job was to pull up close to the building and provide immediate support and cover from the constant fire so that the SEALs could safely evacuate.

We rolled up as near to the building as we could, all of us riding safely inside the strong armor of the Bradley. By this time, we had learned not to ride with our upper half exposed like we had done just months before, instead staying ensconced in the hatch of the Bradley. Our dismounts wasted no time in exiting the vehicle as soon as we slowed to a stop and began to establish a security perimeter. I prepared to make my exit just after theirs, but as I did, all hell broke loose. Constant fire surrounded the Bradley, prohibiting me from stepping out of the top of the vehicle without the immediate risk of being shot. My gunner was already heavily engaged, which meant that I also couldn't exit the rear of the Bradley, due to the exit's position, without him losing the ability to scan and shoot. I stayed inside and shouted orders from the radio, promising the men that I'd meet up with them as soon as there was a break in fire. I awaited my chance to exit, my heart pounding. For a brief moment, the fire seemed to die down and I saw my chance. I opened the hatch and stood about halfway up, when suddenly a figure darted around the corner and fired an RPG directly at me. The shot went wide, but I dove back into the Bradley. My driver, Sergeant Grant, looked in my direction and simply said, "Sir, that's the dumbest fuckin' thing I've ever seen." We both cracked up. I knew he was right, there was no smart or safe way for me to exit the vehicle at this point. But I continued to wait for my moment to dismount, not wanting to remain in the vehicle while my men were on the outside.

I sensed another opportunity just a little while later and took it. I made it out of the vehicle, but had to run about one hundred meters along a fence to reach the building's entrance. The inner football player in me kicked into high gear and I sprinted with everything in me. Shots fired from across the street and exploded all around. Adrenaline poured through my system. My breathing came in rapid spurts, until finally I made it safely to the breezeway between two buildings where my men were positioned. I exhaled a momentary sigh of relief.

The SEALs made their way down from the second floor to join us in the breezeway. But as they did, we began to receive an onslaught of fire from the building next to us. The enemy had higher ground and a perfect vantage point to fire on our exposed position in the breezeway. It seemed that shooters occupied every window beside us. Only a few pillars were available to provide cover, and we stayed hidden behind them as the barrage of constant fire poured in. We were pinned down from all sides. And we had to fight back.

I devised a quick plan with one of my men. Our visibility was blocked, so we couldn't see which windows were occupied by shooters, making it an inefficient guessing game when returning fire. To remedy this, we each took turns jumping into the open and firing a couple of shots to elicit return fire from one of the window shooters. Meanwhile, the other one watched carefully for the location of the return shot and fired back. With this tactic, we started gaining a better idea of which rooms the shooters were in, so I radioed the Bradley and informed them of this knowledge so that they could join us in retaliation.

The Bradley wasted no time coming to our aid. As it approached, it unleashed its 25mm rounds into the building. The sight of this unchecked firepower completely took my breath away. Shards of destruction tore through the sides of the building with unrelenting force. There was something so powerful, so beautiful about it all. Even in the midst of all the chaos, I just stopped, and the two men at my side did the same. Our weapons dropped to our sides and we stood there paralyzed in intense amazement, soaking in the sight before us. We were completely vulnerable and exposed, weapons at our sides, but somehow the awe of it wiped away every thought of danger. It is strangely alluring watching that much firepower lay into a structure at such close range. The sheer imposition of our power, our will onto that of the enemy—it sent an electric thrill through me. Destruction by utter, magnificent force is a thing to behold. And we gaped at the majesty of it unfolding before our eyes. I turned to the sergeant beside me, whose face showed the awe we both felt. "Holy shit, that was cool" were the only words we could find.

The threat from the window shooters next door was completely eliminated, but as soon as it stopped, a man from the slums behind the building began chunking grenades in our direction. At first the grenades weren't landing near enough to really worry us, but they drew closer and closer, soon threatening to do some real damage. We tried to fire back at him, but he was well hidden.

"If he's going to throw grenades at us, let's throw some back at him!" I yelled over the endless string of explosions. So we began throwing grenades, one after another, but none reached our target and we were running out. "Guys, someone has to go out in the open and throw one of these!" I shouted. "The rest of us can provide cover."

"I'll do it, but I'm out of grenades!" one of the men shouted back. "Does anyone have one?"

"I do!" I yelled, handing mine to him. He took it, and after a running start threw it with all of his might. But the grenade didn't make it out of the breezeway, instead striking a lip that hung down from the roof and bouncing off. I watched in sickened horror as it started rolling back towards us. A moment of panic washed over me, but it was accompanied by a sort of slow-motion clarity. Most of the men were facing out, completely unaware of the approaching grenade about to detonate in a matter of seconds. The sergeant who threw it sprinted away as it headed straight for me, and someone yelled, "Grenade!" Two of my men were still facing away from the incoming danger, directly in the line of fire. I took off running in their direction and towards the grenade, moments later skidding up to my men. I roughly grabbed them and yanked them with all my strength behind a nearby pillar and dove behind it myself. No time to brace for the explosion. As soon as we landed, the grenade detonated on the other side.

Shouts rang out over the booming of the repeated explosions landing near us, a chaotic blend of loud voices asking if anyone was hurt. "I'm hit, I'm hit!" someone yelled. It was Specialist Michael Roggero. He had taken off running when the grenade exploded, but a piece of shrapnel still caught him in the leg. A swarm of men surrounded him, trying to assess the damage while others yelled at everyone to take cover as the explosions continued to get closer. We then realized that two men from the scout platoon that had come along to help protect the SEALs were injured, as well as another man by the name of Chris Killion. With four men wounded, we knew that we had to get out of there as soon as possible. But the hits just kept coming.

Somehow without detection, a car loaded with a bomb snuck past our rear-formed security. The car roared into view and slammed into one of our Bradleys with two of our commanders inside. The Bradley was positioned right in the middle of our formation and the impact sent off a devastating explosion, only fifty meters from where I stood. The detonation threw me into the metal railing behind me. I pulled myself up from where I fell, pain shooting through my back, and looked up to see hot flames raging in a feverish orange glow as the Bradley caught on fire. Men rushed toward it and opened the top of the burning vehicle to rescue those within. They successfully pulled the men out, but those inside were already wounded. The situation was escalating rapidly and getting exponentially worse. We already had four men hurt by the grenade and now those pulled from the burning Bradley were added to our number of injured. But war is merciless and we continued to be pelted with a constant onslaught of fire.

We began the evacuation process, trying to navigate the danger of each incoming hit as best as possible. Finally, most of the men had made it safely to the vehicles and only a small group remained, including me. Michael Roggero was able to walk, despite his injuries, but Chris Killion was visibly struggling. I hurried over and supported him, straining slightly under the searing pain in my back, and we headed toward the Bradley, hoping to God that we wouldn't get hit while en route. A small relief swelled through me as I placed Chris in the back of the Bradley and hopped in beside him. We all breathed deeply as we settled within the safety of its strong walls and rumbled away. Time began to slow, along with our breathing, the farther we drove.

In moments like that, the world goes from speeding past you in a whirling fog, your adrenaline and sheer will to survive providing you with an instinctual clarity of mind and the ability to make hundreds of snap decisions, to a sudden, complete quiet as the pulse slows and adrenaline drains. There's so much you could talk about, so much you could say, so much for the mind to process, but it's hard to find words. A young, quiet soldier who sat beside me simply said, "Holy shit, we were on point today." And we all nodded.

As we drove, one of the injured men seemed to be struggling excessively for having sustained only a small hole in his leg from shrapnel, and we grew increasingly worried. We finally made it back to base and rapidly delivered the wounded men to the hospital. I waited on the sidelines inside the CSH (Combat Support Hospital) with another man from the scout platoon as the medics swung into action. The injured man who had been struggling so much was still writhing in pain, and from our vantage point just outside of his room we watched the medics swiftly cut his pants open as he laid on the table. It was obvious that something wasn't right, his face twisted in pain and blood covered him.

"His condition seems to be getting worse," I remarked to the man beside me, wondering what was wrong. But as the nurse grabbed a handful of the injured man's exposed manhood in preparation to insert a catheter—common procedure in these situations—he momentarily forgot his dire condition, a look of fear and anger overtaking him. Here was a man who had just endured the pain of very real combat and had resiliently stood strong in the face of injury. He hadn't blinked at the sight of his own blood soaking through his uniform from the shrapnel that had carved a hole in his flesh. But the moment he saw that catheter, he began to squirm and loudly protest like nothing else: "GET THAT FUCKIN' THING OUT OF MY DICK!"

I smiled at my buddy next to me. Because that's the funny thing about war and combat—sometimes it's not the adrenaline-packed moments of danger, or even the searing pain of an injury, that make a soldier holler the loudest. Instead, it's the tiny tube they try to push inside your privates that causes the most distress. We received word not long after that the piece of shrapnel had started making its way to his heart, and that's why his condition had gone from bad to worse so quickly. The situation almost claimed his life. Thankfully, he made it through. Even the tiniest of wounds can prove to be life threatening and that was a sobering reality we all had to face.

We made the way back to our home at the international base after making sure that our men were in stable condition in the hospital. As the excitement and adrenaline wore off, a deep weariness overtook me. I filled out my debrief, recounting the events of the day as they had happened. We caught word that things on Haifa street and Talial Square were still in total chaos and we were ordered to stand by our vehicles in case we got called out again. We had been awake since midnight, and the indescribable exhaustion that follows the high of combat hit us all like the proverbial ton of bricks.

Dressed in our full gear, we all laid out on the asphalt next to our vehicles and just passed out. The scalding sun burned down on us, but we didn't even notice. We slipped into a deep sleep that remains one of the sweetest slumbers I have ever experienced. We didn't get called back out that day, but we stayed by our vehicles, ready to jump into action again if needed.

As the day drew to a close and everything stilled and quieted, I filled my starving belly with food. The day's events played through my head like a movie on a constant loop. In the moment while the battle rages, there is a clarity of mind and a sort of blind trust you place in the decisions you make while under fire. You devise a strategy and then wholeheartedly run with it, trusting that your training has equipped you for those moments. But later, when all is quiet and the stomach is full and the pulse throbs at its normal beat, you run through every choice, every decision, second guessing yourself. Wondering if it was right or wrong, wondering if you did everything you could have. I turned over each second of the day in my head, analyzing my performance; I carefully took inventory of every call I made and command I gave. But after rolling it over in my mind again and again, I realized with satisfaction that, if given it all to do over, I'd probably do it just about the same way. My men and I had done well in a tough situation and that made me proud. Then came thoughts of all the people who had poured into me to make me the kind of man who was prepared for a day like the one I had just faced. My football coach, toughening me up… Adam and Moose, teaching me to think on my feet and improvise in difficult situations… my mom's resilience in hard circumstances, which I had witnessed all throughout my childhood—I felt thankful for everyone who invested in me.

A few months later, two of our men received Silver Stars for their act of valor in pulling the injured men out of the burning

Bradley. I received a Bronze Star With Valor for placing myself in danger to return fire on the window shooters and for running through the path of the grenade, pulling two of my men to safety. And that will forever remain one of the proudest days of my life.

But only days after the events of September 12th, while the charge from the battle still glowed within us, we received the count of dead women and children who were inside the building that the Bradley had fired on. The insurgents chose to take over rooms where innocent women and children lived, placing their lives in danger as they used these areas to fire on us, leaving us no choice but to defend ourselves. I recalled the Bradley firing on that building, its sheer power so violently displayed, and how it caused me to drop my weapon at my side. The moment had been electric as I watched us so mightily overpower the enemy. But as we read the report of women and children whose lives were suddenly ended that day, we saw the gruesome toll taken by the beautiful force of war.

While I scanned the report, there was a strange void of feeling inside of me. An unsettling realization began to sink in. I was changing. This constant onslaught of evil violence that we were tasked with pushing back against every day was slowly but surely searing the nerve endings of my heart and soul, making it nearly impossible for me to feel or be touched by emotion or empathy when faced with the brutal truths of this war that I fought. Although I held the reports of those dead, though I looked at the gory pictures of that day that were released through the media for the world to see, though my mind registered the atrocity of it all, I felt nothing.

I was not the man I used to be.

Chapter 6

"We sleep safely in our beds because rough men stand ready in the night to visit violence on those who would harm us."—Unknown

Tired. That was the only word that could adequately sum up my feelings in October of 2004. Experiencing an onslaught of constant harassment when we ventured out had long since become routine. It's a funny thing how it all becomes normal... the shooting, the being shot at, the minor injuries. Sometimes I thought back to the day when I saw that black smoke swirling up from those tires and experienced my first twenty seconds of real combat and the effect that it had on me. So much had changed since then. Now these encounters had become nothing more than a typical day's work. But it still took its toll on all of us. The excitement and rush was still there when situations heated up and became dangerous, but it didn't last as long. The crash came sooner and sooner each time now. I didn't sleep more than three hours straight during those months. I might accumulate nine hours of sleep in a twenty-four-hour period, but it would be comprised of several shorter naps combined. And though I tried my best to push it far from my mind, the fact that a broken marriage awaited me at home weighed heavily on me. From the combination of it all, a deep, unmistakable weariness began to sink in. The almost daily adrenaline highs of engaging a hateful enemy, followed by the unavoidable crash into exhaustion, wears on the body.

Not long into October, my platoon went out for our normal patrol near Haifa Street once again. Although the summer temperatures had abated slightly, it was still very hot. We had received a call that something was stirring and we were ordered to check it out, so we loaded up and headed into the blistering sunshine. We walked near the structures we called the hotel series, which were residential buildings, offering downtown condominium living just outside the international zone. These seventeen-story buildings stood tall against the bright Iraqi sun above Haifa Street. We were not far from the location where we had positioned the SEAL team just a few weeks ago and the events of September 12th had taken place. The buildings towered upward impressively, providing a large distraction of sorts from the horrible slums that lay just behind them. On the ground floor of each was an open area, a breezeway, with a series of columns and arched entryways at the edges forming something like a repeated pattern of the letter 'm'. In this very urban environment, the only greenery in sight was the line of palm trees planted in the median of the road running past, along with a handful of other trees in a patch of grass fronting the condos. An alley ran behind the buildings, where a six- or seven-foot wall separated them from the slums that stretched for miles. I walked with a small group of my men past the buildings, near the square, while the others patrolled nearby.

The silence was broken by an all too familiar sound, a faint metallic 'ping' that signified someone had released the spoon, or safety lever, of a grenade. We had all heard this countless times—I stopped counting at two hundred in my first month and a half—and knew what was coming. Seconds later, the burst of exploding grenades pounded our eardrums due to the close range, and we saw dust rising up from the other side of the buildings, near the slums. One of our squads was under attack. The string of grenades was followed by gunfire, and moments later a call came through on my radio from SSG John Jacobson, one of my squad leaders.

"I'm hit again," he said, "and Towne got hit, it looks pretty bad."

We needed to get to them as soon as possible. I looked around, rapidly determining our best route, but the path toward their location placed us right out in the open—in clear view of those firing over the wall, where the attacks were coming from.

We quickly devised a plan. We spread out, seven men wide, and began walking down the street towards the other squad, our hands placed on our triggers, unloading a constant, furious stream of fire against the wall where the enemy was concealed. We knew that we might not hit anyone, but at the very least it was a way to provide cover for ourselves due to the fact that they wouldn't risk popping up to throw a grenade our way while a wall of bullets poured in their direction. It was one of the most exhilarating moments in combat that I had ever experienced, standing side-by-side with my fellow soldiers, sending hundreds of bullets ripping through the air, creating a line of fire like none other I had seen.

It worked, and we were able to close the distance between us and our other men, who had retreated from danger into the nearest building's open ground floor. As we reached the breezeway, Sergeant Towne, a good buddy of mine, came into my view. Bright red blood spurted out from his neck, pouring down his face and cheek. His hand grasped furiously at the fountain of blood pulsing out of him. As soon as I saw that flood of crimson, a jolt of panic shot through me.

"They got me again, sir," Sergeant Towne said, as calm as he could be. But I feared that his jugular vein had been hit.

We had to medically evacuate, and I looked around to assess our options. There were several others wounded as well and I couldn't risk trying to transport these injured men by evacuating them the same way that we had gotten here, back down the alley and around to the main road. Using a hail of bullets as protection had worked before, but would undoubtedly be much harder with wounded men in tow. Directly in front of us was a small parking lot, filled with cars. There was no open space for a Bradley to pull in close. But as I looked back down at the injured man by my side, I knew exactly what had to be done. I radioed the Bradley: "Look, I don't care what you have to knock down or run over, I need you to pull up right to where I'm standing and drop the fucking ramp right where my feet are, and I need you to do it now."

My men in the Bradley didn't say a word, they just gunned the engines. With a roar, the Bradley thundered toward us, straight over the cars in the parking lot. The parked vehicles screeched in protest as the weight of the Bradley crushed them, one after another. I marveled at the sound and sight of total destruction as the Bradley stopped at nothing in its path toward the wounded man by my side. It halted and the ramp dropped at my feet, just as I had asked. We wasted no time in loading up the injured men, who were taken straight to the hospital.

The rest of us finished the mission, staying to do what was needed and hoping the wounded had received the care they needed to survive. As soon as possible, I headed to the hospital to check on my men. There, my fears were put to rest; although the men had been pelted with shrapnel, they were stable and were going to be alright, even Sergeant Towne. Everyone would make a full recovery. And that made it a good day in our book.

Experiences like these were becoming somewhat average rather than extraordinary like they used to be. The fighting was constant. It wasn't uncommon to be grazed by small pieces of shrapnel during these fights, and our barometer for what constituted a true injury had been altered through constant exposure to combat situations. One day, while my platoon investigated an abandoned building, an RPG impacted outside, and glass blasted into the room where we stood. As I dove to the ground, my arm was sliced by a flying shard. Later, several guys prodded me to see the medics about it.

"You need to get that looked at," one of the men in my platoon said, and others nodded in agreement. "You can get put in for a Purple Heart."

"Are you kidding?" I said. "You know how silly I'd feel going in for a cut on my arm?"

My platoon sergeant actually submitted the paperwork to put me in for a Purple Heart, but when I went to see my company commander he laughed and said there was no way in hell he was putting me in for it. I wholeheartedly agreed. Even if I were given a Purple Heart, I'd never be able to look at it without feeling a sense of shame. Our platoon had already received more Purple Hearts than any other platoon in our company. But many of us struggled because all Purple Hearts were not equal. One man takes a piece of shrapnel to the brain and another gets a cut from flying debris and needs stitches, and they both constitute a Purple Heart. We began to laugh in the face of the smaller scrapes, cuts, and bruises of combat, and it became somewhat of a running joke as we would tell whoever was hurt something along these lines: "Toughen up! A little scrape like that is nothing to cry about, and certainly nothing to get a Purple Heart for."

One day, we were tasked with guarding a set of alleyways in a notoriously bad part of town. We were in charge of keeping anything dangerous from coming out of the slum area to the main road. There were murmurings of danger and problems arising that day, but I hadn't seen anything yet and so my men and I pushed forward. We set up on the northwest part of Talial Square, where the buildings were around seven to nine stories tall, and we sought out positions that offered proper fields of fire on likely ingresses for the enemy while still providing decent cover.

I stopped for a moment when I found a good vantage point for one of my men to set up and wait, a small wall on the backside of a building, facing the alleyway. I called Chris Killion over. Chris was tall and funny, from Detroit, a smart-ass but the exact person you want with you when the shit goes down. I'd be lying if I said he wasn't one of my favorites.. "This is a good place for you to set up and stay," I told him. "I need you to focus down this alley."

"Sir, are you fuckin' crazy?" he joked. "Are you trying to get me my second Purple Heart?"

I laughed. He had just been injured during the events of September 12th. As I began to walk away, I called back, "After that little scratch you got last time, if you want me to put you in for another Purple Heart you better lose a leg or something!" And then, as if on cue, a fraction of a second after the words passed my lips, a grenade came flying over the wall from the other side of the alley and blew up right next to Chris.

He sustained significant injuries. Another of my men began lobbing grenades to provide cover, and I grabbed Chris and dragged him into the breezeway. As soon as the medics arrived, I handed him over and went back to assess the circumstances for the rest of my platoon. The situation was under control. A few minutes later I hurried back to check on Chris, who felt well enough to promptly cuss me out, which

I took as a good sign. He was medically evacuated and taken to a hospital for care.

A few hours later, when the fight died down, I was able to go and check on him. I walked into his room and found him lying bandaged on a hospital bed, talking to his mom on the phone. "Mom, mom, hold on just a second," he said over the phone as he saw me enter. "The asshole responsible for all of this just walked in. Do you want to say hi to him?"

I started laughing and shook my head, and then he broke out into laughter right along with me. It turned out that he didn't actually lose his leg as I had prophesied over him, but he did sustain a terrible injury from the incident, later causing him to be medically boarded out of the Army. He never walked the same again. When you deal with that much combat, that much proximity to the threat of death, that much blood, you have to find a way to keep your cool. And making light of an otherwise terrible situation is one of the only ways to do that.

October of 2004 remains in my mind as a braid of memories: of the hot Iraqi sun, the sound of exploding grenades, the rush of adrenaline, and the tired relief of ending the day with each of my men alive, ready to face another day. Those weeks run together in a fuzzy haze of exhilaration and exhaustion. But some memories emerge from that fog in sharp relief.

One such memory took place during that October while my platoon was on patrol. We walked through an area called Sheikh Marouf Circle near an above-ground cemetery. Rotting trash piles lined the streets and mixed with the smell of the cemetery, the stench far more unbearable than usual. I was in front as we walked, my men following behind me. Without warning, a grenade exploded toward the back of our group. Instinctively, my men bringing up the rear turned around with guns ready just as two men popped into view. My men fired. Two bodies instantly dropped, falling lifelessly into the trash piled along the street. We followed typical protocol and quickly marched up to a nearby rooftop to gain a good vantage point of the area. Once I could clearly assess our surroundings and gauge any other potential threats, I told the Bradleys to pull in closer to provide protection and commanded my men to set up on different corners to establish a safe perimeter. I then ordered Corporal Burgess and the medic to come with me, one to handle radio communications and the other to evaluate the condition of the two men that were shot.

As we approached, the picture in front of us was gruesome. One man appeared to be dead, his misshapen face planted in the garbage, a huge hole in his head exposing the interior of his skull. His brains had splattered across the trash. The other man had been hit in the hip and was still alive, thrashing and screaming. The medic strode quickly toward the hurting man and I ordered him to patch him up. We would try to stabilize his condition and bring him back with us, in hopes that he could provide us with intel.

"Corpy, call in and let HQ know that we were engaged and returned fire," I told Corporal Burgess. "Give them our location. Tell them we've got one enemy KIA and one enemy WIA. Tell them we're working on getting the WIA patched up and sent back to the hospital, hopefully to provide some intel." Corporal Burgess relayed the message. But no sooner had he pronounced one man WIA (Wounded In Action) and one man KIA (Killed In Action) than a horrible, almost inhuman moaning arose from the man with the gaping hole in his head. I looked down in horror at the gory mess that lay in front of me, wondering how a sound could possibly be rising from it. The man strained to lift his neck, his face still planted in the pile of trash, causing blood to pour from the hole in his head. I froze and shot a look toward Corpy whose expression mirrored my own. "Well, maybe you need to make that two enemy WIAs," I said. Corpy radioed in the correction, but as he did the man fell silently back down into the trash with a thud of finality. "Never mind," I said. "Tell them to keep him as KIA." I watched as the medic continued to work on the man who had taken a bullet to the hip.

And then again, that bone-chilling, guttural groan rose from the direction of the mangled head that lay amidst the garbage. I looked over and saw something I can never forget. The man had moved his arm up, stuck his fingers into the hole in his head, and pulled his head up out of the trash. The stomach-turning groan began again as he lifted up his destroyed face, causing blood and brains to pour from the hole and down his face and cheek. "Holy Shit," were the only words that came out of my mouth as the gruesome scene unfolded. The medic ran over and began to attend to the man, and we placed a trash bag under his bloody head before loading both men in the Bradley and transporting them back to the hospital. Incredibly, the man with a hole in his head actually lived for a few days.

That incident was a turning point for me, as I realized that some things can never be unseen. In that moment of staring down at the man laying gruesomely in the garbage, I took note of my reaction, and it was like watching once-burned, deadened fingertips grasp at red-hot iron. The mind registers that some intense feeling should arise, some reaction of revolt, but nothing is felt. As I stood there amidst the stench of trash and the sight of horror, it hit me that nothing seemed out of place. It was just another day. I felt nothing at all. And I knew that reacting this way was not a good thing, but I had no idea how to reverse the shift within me.

Not long after, we went out once again, accompanied by a small team of SEALs with orders to occupy Talial Square. This was also a very urban area, with tall buildings and a mosque on one corner of the square. If we were not present, this was usually one of the busiest intersections in

Baghdad—plenty of cars, pedestrians, vendors, stalls, and people selling or cooking or buying. But if we were there, nearly everyone cleared out, closing up shop and making themselves scarce. We would park our Bradleys, dismount and set up, and secure the perimeter.

For this particular mission, it was mid-afternoon and hot as hell. Like anything, we had learned to adjust to the heat over time, but still it wore on us. We had men up on the 7th and 8th floors of buildings that stood in four corners of Talial Square, but only two buildings had SEALs in them. The SEALs were the designated shooters. I was with a group in a building without SEALs, and we were tasked with being the lookouts. We occupied an empty condo for this mission, and we stood in the living room and took positions near the windows. We watched and waited but nothing happened.

Abruptly, movement caught our eyes and we strained to get a better look from our vantage point. We watched a kidnapping took place right in front of us. We stood there, shocked onlookers, while several vehicles pulled up on all sides of a local Iraqi who was sitting in his car. A group of insurgents poured out of the vehicles, pointing their guns at the man, ordering him out of the car. Up until this point, we hadn't received permission to engage, and I remained quieter than usual due because my direct superior was on the mission that day, though in a different building, and I knew he would take lead on communication with HQ. I listened as he called in and described the events that we were watching unfold in front of us, asking for permission to engage.

The answer came back over the radio, straight to the point: "Granted."

Two of the SEALs fired their weapons on the insurgents below as the kidnapping progressed. They hit a few of them, but the others acted fast, loading their wounded as well as the kidnapping victim in their vehicle and driving away. By firing the shots, we had just declared ourselves. The events of September 12th were fresh in all of our minds and we knew the danger that could ensue if our position was discovered and the enemy decided to surround our buildings. We all felt on edge, hoping our location wouldn't be found out. Despite the danger of having declared our presence, we decided to stay in hopes that a big group might come out in pursuit of us and we'd be able to hit them hard from our protected vantage point. Everyone was prepared to engage and fire if need be.

Activity on the street began to increase, and we watched and waited tensely. My viewpoint wasn't ideal, so I craned my head for a better look at what was going on. A group seemed to be gathering below, and I radioed in, "I think I'm seeing a group forming here." I strained to see closer.

"I think you're right, we see it too," Company Commander Jason Bennett radioed back. "What are they doing?"

"I think they are pointing," I said.

"Yeah, I see that, too."

"No, umm, I think they are pointing at us!" My voice rose with alarm as more men joined the threatening group below.

Jason Bennett had a dry, witty sense of humor, and it wasn't lost to him even in a tense moment such as this.

"Well," he said, and chuckled over the radio, "good luck, dude."

My men and I stood behind the windows, looking out, trying to get a handle on the quickly evolving situation. It appeared that word had gotten out, mistakenly, that our building was the one that housed the sniper that had just fired shots against the enemy, and now we were in the crosshairs of direct retaliation. An odd sense of danger came over the whole area as the streets began to empty out and we knew from experience that something was about to happen. We braced for it. Unbeknownst to us, one enemy sniper and a man with a machine gun had taken position and were aiming directly for the window where we stood. I peeked my head cautiously around the curtain framing the window for a glimpse of the street and then withdrew. In a fraction of a second, a shot from the sniper fired through the window. By pure luck, I had pulled my head back just before the bullet whizzed past. It was the closest call I ever had. We all froze. And then another single shot fired. And then another.

"Holy Shit!" we yelled as we dove for cover. No sooner had we landed than bullets came pumping into the room, unloading with rapid force from the machine gun. We all began to low crawl as quickly as we could from the living room toward the hallway and back bedrooms, hoping to gain better protection from the continuous fire and the threat of ricocheting bullets. The condo wasn't large, and we found whatever spot we could to take cover. I was the farthest from the hallway, so by the time I wiggled my way across the floor, men had already filled it. There was a tiny bathroom with just a sink and a toilet off to the side, so I made my way in there. I shimmied across the bathroom floor and maneuvered behind the toilet, in the thin space between it and the wall, hoping to at the very least protect my head. The sound was deafening as bullets shot into the room by the hundreds, intermittently mixed with the roar of the sniper rifle, even louder as it fired single shots. The ammunition pelted the walls, tearing a path of destruction. The sniper's rifle shots left an especially impressive signature, creating large holes in the walls around us. In the midst of this chaos I radioed in to my company commander, telling him what was going on. He ordered me to sit tight and that the cavalry was on its way. They would be arriving with as many vehicles as possible and would clear the building floor by floor until they could reach us.

And so we stayed low and we waited. A small break in the constant fire finally came and everything went quiet for a few seconds. We didn't move a muscle; we hardly dared to breathe. Just as relief prepared to settle in, another onslaught of bullets came crashing into the room. This continued steadily for what felt like an eternity... in actuality, probably only five to seven minutes. None of us dared to move. Until someone came through the door to rescue us, we weren't going to risk getting up. Eventually, the firing stopped and we found ourselves enveloped in total silence again. One of my men peeked in the bathroom where I lay with my head awkwardly behind the toilet.

Suddenly, he broke the silence. "Sir, did you ever think you'd be taking cover behind a shitter?" The room erupted with a chorus of laughter from all the men. The jokes started flying and then a series of hilarious stories as we waited for the cavalry to arrive. We lay there laughing like hysterical schoolgirls for a good thirty to forty-five minutes. It was as if the stress and adrenaline that pumped through our bodies burst out like a can of shaken soda in those peals of laughter. Eventually, reinforcements came and helped us safely make our way to the rooftop while we waited for more vehicles to arrive. I walked out on the rooftop, took a seat against a wall, and rested the back of my head against it. The rush of excitement from the incident drained from me, and coupled with the massive release of emotion from the laughter, I felt utterly worn out. I looked at the three men who had plopped down next to me, and their drooping shoulders and facial expressions echoed everything I felt. Just total, pure exhaustion.

In November, I got the chance to take leave and fly back to the states for fourteen days. I slept for hours on the plane back home. My mom picked me up from Fort Walton Beach Airport in Florida when I arrived, a small regional airport. It was so good to see a familiar face, even better that it was my kind and thoughtful mom, and she immediately wrapped me in a huge hug. Once we got in the car, it was clear that she wanted to give her son anything that was needed, but she wasn't certain what that was. After a moment of silence, she tried to lighten the mood. "Do you want me to buy you a six-pack, son? Or I can stop at the strip club for you? What do you need?"

I laughed. "No, I'm good, Mom." I was just ready to see friends and family and relax.

I met up with Crissy briefly to retrieve my wallet and we exchanged very few words. I don't think either of us knew what to say. In the following days, I connected with friends and family and went out for drinks almost every night. The first question everyone asks is, "What is it like over there?" But I didn't mind answering. I enjoyed getting to share stories and pictures and recount the high points of my experience. I stayed away from the more disturbing details and didn't let on to the aspects of the job that were tiring or had begun to take a toll on my mind and emotions.

My buddies seemed to have the pulse on what I needed. They would ask me a few questions and let me share about my experiences, and then sensed my desire to kick back and relax after that initial conversation, getting my mind off of the subjects that had consumed me for months. I had no shortage of drinking buddies to help me do just that. On one particular night, I met up with a group of friends from college at Penny Beer Bar, our old college stomping grounds, on karaoke night. We sat there for hours, talking and drinking. Suddenly my buddy Scott, a rather impressively large fellow, rose from the table with a look in his eye that I couldn't quite pinpoint. He strode over to the karaoke machine where a small frat boy stood holding the mic, ready to sing a song.

"Hand me the mic," Scott said, towering over the scared-looking boy. The kid just stared back, wordless. With one swoop, Scott grabbed the mic from the boy's hand and spoke into it. "I just want you all to know that my closest friend in the world, Jeff Morris here, is on leave from Iraq. This guy is over there getting shot at every day just so people like us can go out and have a good time tonight. So if he doesn't have a shot and a drink in front of him the rest of the night, I'm going to kick each and every one of your goddamn asses!" And then he threw the mic on the floor and walked off.

It wasn't even a minute before I had people lining up at the bar to shake my hand and thank me for my service. My glass wasn't empty for the rest of the night. Scott was a dedicated wingman and made sure to tell any of the girls who approached just how much danger I was in, adding in the sad, cheesy line, "He may never have the chance to be with a woman again." I just laughed at these well-meaning but pitiful attempts he made on my behalf. I wasn't interested in bringing anyone home; I just wanted to spend time with my friends. But you can't blame a good buddy for trying. We went out Friday and Saturday night and had a blast, drinking far more than we probably should have.

On Sunday I prepared to drive back to my parents' home, more than a little hung over. My Aunt Heidi called and asked me to come by her house, which was about an hour away, and I told her I'd try to make it. But I didn't feel well, I was exhausted from the late nights, and the weather was horrible, so I called and told her I wasn't up for a visit after all. But her voice took on a serious tone and she simply said, "No, you're going to come here before you head back."

I didn't argue. After arriving at my aunt's house, we exchanged hellos, but then they grew somber. "We need to tell you something, Jeff," Aunt Heidi said.

My Uncle Scott, who is a surgeon, leaned forward in his chair and spoke calmly. "Your mom has discovered that she has a brain aneurysm that hasn't ruptured, but could at any time. She's scheduled for brain surgery in just a couple of days."

He let this sink in as I sat there, reeling, no response coming from me. After a moment, he continued. "She didn't want to tell you until you got back to Iraq so that you wouldn't worry. But we feel that you should know in case things don't go well."

"I'll ask to extend my leave," I said. "I'll stay and see her through the surgery."

My aunt and uncle agreed that this was the right thing to do, but before I left my aunt had one more thing on her mind: "I don't know all the details of what happened with you and Crissy, but marriage is a big deal. It's something you have to work for and fight for. Don't just bail on it. You have a little time before the surgery, and I have airline miles that need to be used. Take them and fly to Austin and see Crissy. Try to work things out." Once again, I didn't argue.

I immediately requested an extension of my leave in order to stay for my mother's surgery, and I received permission. Following my aunt's prompting, I spent a few days with Crissy, and in that short time we rekindled what little was left of our relationship. We parted with a promise between us to try and work things out when I got back home. Then it was time for my mom's surgery, and I sat anxiously in the waiting room of the hospital as the procedure was carried out. Eventually, the good news was relayed to me—my mother made it through the surgery without complication. Relief flooded through me. In the recovery room, my mom was so thankful to have me there.

Before I knew it, my extended leave time was up. I packed, headed for the airport, and boarded the plane to Iraq. I arrived back in Iraq on the 10th of December and hit the ground running as if I had never left.

Thankfully, the frequency of the attacks that we had once constantly experienced was steadily slowing down. We felt an incredible sense of pride and accomplishment in that fact, knowing that all those days of fighting and risking our lives were beginning to pay off. Christmas and New Year's Day came and were much like any other day; we went out on patrol and then returned to open whatever care packages we had been sent from home, which turned out to be a big hodge-podge from different people. Around that time, Under Armour was becoming very popular, and the father of one of the soldiers in my platoon had sent one of their tee-shirts for everybody, nice ones that wicked away sweat, along with a stack of *Playboy* and *Penthouse* magazines. We all agreed that was a great dad.

As we made our way into the early part of 2005, it was becoming more and more obvious just how much things had changed in the region. The truth began to sink in that we had actually cleaned up Haifa Street. In the latter part of January, we prepared to aid in the first Iraqi election since the invasion. It was a proud moment to be a part of this broken country taking steps to rebuild itself. We were out in full force on Election Day, providing security and watching as everyone who voted received an ink stamp on his or her finger. It was almost surreal seeing people go out to vote on Haifa Street, an action that would have been unthinkable just a few months before. We had only a matter of weeks left before we made the handoff to the guys coming to take our place so we could head home. And we felt damn good about the way we were leaving things. There had been a lot of literal blood, sweat, and tears involved in the process of stabilizing the area, but it was worth it. We were scheduled to head home in mid-March and we felt relieved knowing that we were on the home stretch.

But on February 19th, I logged into my military email account and saw an email simply titled, "Adam." It was from Lindsay Malson, my good friend Adam Malson's wife. It read:

Jeff, I'm sorry to have to do this. I know we've never met, but I know that you and Adam became very close during your training and he spoke of you all the time. I'm sorry to let you know that Adam was killed today.

I sat there stunned. Adam was stationed only five to seven miles away from where I was, but we weren't allowed to cross sectors so we hadn't seen each other while in Iraq. I had witnessed wounds and death, and I knew men who had been killed during my time in Iraq, but this was different. Adam was a good friend. He taught me so much, and we shared so many memories. My mind filled with the image of his face and a rush of memories from our days training together in IOBC. We spooned each other on cold nights during our training, we had shared countless bottles of Jack Daniels at one another's homes, we sat across the dinner table sharing food and laughter, we went to church together, we truly become close friends. I stared at that computer screen, not knowing how to reply. I went outside and just started walking. For so long, I felt nothing in the face of grief and horror, but now a whole rush of feelings and emotions were swirling together and rising to the surface. Without warning, tears escaped from my eyes, pouring out all the sorrow and loss I felt.

Eventually, I made my way back and found Jason Bennett, my company commander. I told him about the situation and asked if I could have his support to go to the battalion commander and request to go to Adam's service, given our close proximity to the sector where the service would be held. I received permission and my platoon was given orders to drive to that sector as our patrol for the day. Following receipt of these orders, I addressed my men.

"Although things have gotten better, there's always a risk when we go out, and I don't want to put anyone in danger unnecessarily," I said. "There's a minimum amount of personnel and vehicles that we have to take, but I don't want to place anyone in harm's way who doesn't have to go. There's a risk to attend the service, and I know this is a personal matter I'm asking you to join me in." I paused, taking a steadying breath. "If anyone is willing to go with me, raise your hand."

Every hand in the platoon shot up. When the time came, we drove up to the service without incident. My men patiently waited as I attended the ceremony, respecting that it was a personal moment for me. I asked my radio guy, Michael Roggero, if he would mind going with me and taking a few pictures of that day so that I'd have a captured memory to hold onto in the future. He responded, "Sir, you know there's no way I'd ever leave your side."

You can't adequately prepare for what it's like to lose a close friend in combat. I felt a whole range of emotions as we drove back that day. War greedily takes that which is of the highest value in this world, life itself, and lays claim to it without regard for the grief it leaves in its path. I lost a friend. A good woman lost her husband and the entire future they had awaiting them. Parents lost the son whom they had loved and raised since boyhood. There's nothing but emptiness and sadness that arises when you're faced with these facts. We all knew what we were signing up for when we took our oath, when we swore to serve our country to the best of our abilities. I knew there was some silver lining to be found in the knowledge that he died fighting for and protecting something that we all believed in with all of our hearts. But it's hard to find a silver lining when you find yourself simply wishing you could sit down and share a glass of Jack Daniel's with one of your best friends again.

The attacks that we had once faced constantly were now almost nonexistent as the weeks until our departure grew fewer and fewer. We took American flags and raised them in the trash piles that lined the once dangerous streets, the ones we had accurately named Purple Heart Lane and Grenade Alley. There was a sense of resilient hope and victory as we stood openly in the streets, where we once hardly dared to venture out, and raised those flags high. The enemy had given us all they had and we had taken it and fought back harder. There we were, on what had once been the enemy's sacred ground to attack us from, and we stood tall with our American flags flapping in the breeze. The sense of pride was palpable.

As I boarded the plane in mid-March to fly back home, I remembered walking down that ramp when I first arrived; I recalled the mixture of excitement and the deep desire to prove myself as my boot stepped onto Iraqi soil for the first time. And as I took my last step on that soil and boarded the plane, leaving Iraq behind, I knew I wasn't the same man as the one who had arrived. I felt exhausted. Different. And proud. I did what I had come to do.

After my plane landed, I transferred to a waiting bus that drove us to the military ceremony held to honor those of us coming home. The bus dropped us off, and we marched across a field as friends and family waited on the sidelines. A brief ceremony followed and then the reunions with loved ones began. Due to timing and logistical issues, neither Crissy nor my family were able to make it to the ceremony, so no one was waiting for me as we were released to reconnect with our loved ones. I completely understood and felt no ill feelings toward them. But as the rest of my platoon ran to embrace wives, girlfriends, children, siblings, and parents, I stood there by myself, loneliness washing over me. A ring of sweet reunions took place on every side, nearly encircling me. As I stood in that field alone, the moment felt almost symbolic. It struck me that sometimes being in a position of leadership is a lonely thing. And yet, somehow the moment was perfect in its own way. I stood in the middle of that circle, not saying a word, simply soaking in the sight of parents wrapping their arms around their sons, wives pressing their lips lovingly upon the husband they had missed, children screaming "Daddy!" and running with open abandonment into the arms of their father who had made it home safely. I would have missed out on that moment had I been absorbed with my own reunion. Leading these fine men had been a gift and an honor, and though I felt a slight ache in my own heart, I'd never so enjoyed being lonely in my entire life. Then within minutes, a swarm of people surrounded me as men came over with loved ones by their side saying, "Mom, Dad, I want you to meet Jeff Morris. This is the guy who was in charge of us, who led us, and who kept us alive." I shook the hands of proud parents, thankful to have their boy back home safely, and the tiny hands of children, who beamed in the glow of daddy finally being home.

And I walked off the field that day with my head held high.

Chapter 7

"Walk a little slower, Daddy!" said a little child
so small. "I'm following in your footsteps and I
don't want to fall. Sometimes your steps are very
fast, sometimes they're hard to see; So walk a little
slower Daddy, for you are leading me. Someday
when I'm all grown up, you're what I want to be.
Then I will have a little child who'll want to follow
me. And I would want to lead just right, and know
that I was true; So, walk a little slower, Daddy, for
I must follow you!!"—Unknown

Austin TX, 2005

In the days following my return, I attended to a few necessary
duties and then took a month's leave. It can be quite a shift,
going from a dangerous and regimented environment to
being home with very little responsibility for thirty whole
days. In combat, memories are blazed into your mind in
vivid detail. But away from it all, the days blend together
with very few noteworthy happenings. Crissy and I worked
hard to rebuild the relationship that we both desired and
had briefly re-kindled during my leave over the holidays—
and the effort showed. Our relationship stabilized and we
welcomed the renewal.

When my leave came to a close, I returned to my unit at
Ft. Hood. That's when the deck began to shuffle. I left my
position as platoon leader in Alpha Company 1-9 Cav and

became the executive officer to our sister unit, Charlie 1-9. The executive officer (or XO) is second in the chain of command to the company commander. I was excited about the new opportunity and for the fact that I would be working under Company Commander Chris Ford, whom I had the pleasure of serving with during my first deployment. Simply put, Chris Ford was "the man"—tall, good looking, smart, and great at his job. One of the men put it this way: "He's the kind of guy you want to hate because he's so damn good at everything, but somehow you can't help but like him." That about summed Chris up. He was the kind of man that every guy wants to have a beer with and every girl wants to sleep with. I could think of no one better to serve under and learn from.

But the changes didn't stop there. Not long after, Ft. Hood decided to create what they referred to as "Combined Arms Battalions" in preparation for the next deployment. With this change, we would no longer have infantry battalions made up of infantry companies or tank battalions made up of tank companies. Instead, there would be much larger battalions made up of a combination of infantry companies, tank companies, engineer companies, and so on. It was a brilliant plan, but it required a large adjustment in our structure. I had previously been a part of 1-9 CAV, which was an infantry battalion composed of three infantry companies (Alpha, Bravo, and Charlie). Now, I would be a part of a much larger battalion that would be comprised of two infantry companies, two tank companies, an engineer company, a support company, and a headquarters company. They referred to this process as "reflagging". As they made these shifts across the board, the numbers didn't always add up evenly, which meant more changes had to be made. The men from Charlie 1-9 moved over to 1-8 battalion and Charlie 1-9 was officially reflagged into Bravo 1-8. Now our battalion consisted of Alpha 1-8 infantry company, Bravo

1-8 infantry company (which I was a part of), and Charlie 1-8 and Delta 1-8 tank companies.

Now that we were reflagged into Bravo 1-8, our superiors encouraged us to come up with a new name for our company. During my first deployment, Alpha Company 1-9 had been known as "The Annihilators", and we named Charlie 1-9 "Crazy Wolf". Chris Ford and I, as well as a group of men from the company I had been deployed with, all put our heads together to create a new name. We threw out every name in the book but nothing quite seemed to fit. Then Chris Ford spoke up.

"How about 'Legion'?" Around the room, heads nodded in agreement. It was simple but powerful. And just like that... Legion was born.

We were officially reflagged into Bravo 1-8 in July. As the summer went on, our 135-man infantry company dwindled by half as some men shipped off to other bases and others left the Army altogether. In August, Chris was given a thirty-day assignment as an evaluator for an out of state training event. As the XO, I temporarily took command of the company. I had only been a platoon leader for nine months, an XO for three, and was now temporarily serving as company commander. This was an unusually fast timeline. Not a lot went on during that period, and my job primarily consisted of administrative work, including the monthly inventory. As XO, I had been in charge of all the equipment and logistics and I made a name for myself by implementing efficient ways to inventory and track things. Now that I had the opportunity to run things as a fill-in company commander, I utilized these methods and it garnered attention from the battalion commander and his XO. Tracking inventory was the part of the job that no one liked to do, and they appreciated having someone in charge that got the job done right.

Chris returned in August, just as we began hearing rumors of a storm brewing in the gulf, "Hurricane Katrina." As the nation faced the impending devastation that this storm could cause, we got word that we would be sent to New Orleans to help out. Crissy and I were in the process of buying our first house in the suburbs of Austin when the news came, so we delayed closing on the house as I prepared to leave. I was tasked with moving our not-so-little operation to New Orleans, which was quite an ordeal, and we stayed in the area for two weeks. The devastation was unimaginable, and we worked non-stop to stabilize the shattered community. Our job was not to clean up but to maintain order, prevent looting, and provide security. As the XO at the time, I was the logistics guy. This meant making sure our company had the supplies and equipment it needed. It was a bit surreal—here we were, safely back in the U.S., and with the destruction it almost looked like we were in a combat zone again. Houses were in shambles or missing the top story. Debris littered the street, and wrecked furniture was piled by the roadside. On some of the doors, we'd see symbols that had been spray-painted, showing which homes had been cleared, and which had needed a body removed. It was sobering to see the losses that these communities suffered.

Upon returning, Crissy and I completed the purchase of our first home. It wasn't big or fancy, just a cozy starter house. But it was ours and we loved it. I couldn't help but feel relieved that things were going so well between us as we finally settled into the house in October.

During this time, Chris Ford made the decision to say goodbye to the Army for good. He would keep his position until early fall, at which point a replacement would take over command. Unbeknownst to me, he was putting in a word with our superiors that he thought I'd be a great candidate for taking over the job during the company's training period while they selected another company commander for deployment. They agreed.

On October 25th, I officially took command of Bravo Company, 1-8 CAV. The usual ceremony was conducted for the transfer of command, and though there wasn't anything particularly special about it, it meant a lot to me. As the ceremony began, I looked around to see many familiar faces who came to show their support for me. In attendance was pretty much everyone from my platoon, as well as Jason Bennett, the company commander from my first deployment, who was sporting a long beard now that he was out of the military. My soul swelled with gratitude for each and every one of them. It is customary for only the outgoing commander to make a speech at the ceremony, not the incoming one, so I didn't have the chance to publicly thank all those who made such an effort to be there. But I soaked in every word that Chris spoke and I felt proud, knowing that a man I respected so greatly had spoken up for me and felt confident passing the torch for me to carry. To symbolize this, our unit's guidon flag, which Chris carried in, was passed to the battalion commander, who gave it to me. I was honored to accept that flag and all that it represented. As soon as the ceremony was over I rushed to thank the dozens of people who attended.

Once I took command, I immediately started to train the unit up. The memories of Iraq stood fresh in my mind and I wanted my men to be prepared for what they were about to step into. Our numbers grew as more soldiers were added throughout the fall, and I was excited to watch our company expand. However, I couldn't evict one particularly haunting thought from my mind every time I looked into the eyes of a new young soldier. *What if it's him? What if he's the one who doesn't make it back?* Each man was someone's son, husband, or father, and I knew all too well that not everyone would return home alive. Despite this weighty thought that remained fixed in the back of my mind, I loved having the opportunity to prepare my men for all the things I knew they would face once deployed. Also, in December Crissy and I found out that we were expecting a baby, due in early August of the following year, and we were thrilled. Throughout those cold months, as I prepared my men, a small mound appeared around Crissy's waist as our child grew. I watched with eager anticipation for the arrival of this tiny little Morris, but kept myself busy by putting everything into training my men.

One day in December, we created an all-day training event that we called the Legion Squad Competition. The event would last for the majority of the day and would consist of a series of tests. All those who participated would have to work their way through the Army PT test, shooting tests, speed assembly and disassembly of weapons tests, land navigation tests, and more. We planned to start at Ft. Hood and slowly work our way deeper into the woods as the event progressed. The day would end with a mud pit wrestling match, and for this we chose a gigantic sand pit that would be the perfect arena. A group of our men who were injured and unable to participate in the event spent the entire day filling up five-gallon jugs with water, driving out to the sand pit, and emptying the jugs into it. They followed my instructions to get the pit as squishy, slimy, and swampy as possible. The muddy battle would be the grand finale, and I didn't want it to disappoint. We planned the events on paper with great intention: we'd start at 4:30 AM, arrive at the mud pits by 8:00 PM, and then throw a barbecue to finish off the day. But once the event was underway, everything took far longer than expected. Soon we were pushing midnight and we weren't even done. It was cold and the hour grew late, but the guys were having fun. Everyone was tired but in good spirits when we arrived at the mud pit in the wee hours of the morning.

All those participating, plus a handful of guys who came to watch, drove their vehicles out to the pit and circled around it. Someone produced a massive speaker and set it up on the edge of the pit. I pulled out my best heavy-metal/death-metal mixtape, and soon the throbbing beats of the music blared. The headlight beams shone through the fog, illuminating the thick mud, the battle-ready men gathered around, and the rising steam. The ring was ready. The last man standing would be crowned the champion of the day, and every man wanted that to be him. The energy and testosterone were palpable.

All of the officers, including me, had been serving as the judges for the day, which meant we knew what was coming next. The moment we yelled go, the men weren't going to run and attack each other. No, they would be running straight for us and they would do everything in their power to get us as muddy as possible. The scout platoon leader, Charlie Erwin, made a valiant effort to exempt himself.

"Now, listen, I'm only here to watch," he told the gathered group. "I'm driving my wife's car, and it's brand new. I didn't bring a change of clothes. I'm just here to help judge, alright?"

I approached him and put a hand on his shoulder. "Charlie," I said, "When we yell go, you better take off running with everything in you. You know the boys, especially your boys, don't give a damn about your car or clothes. They are going to head right for you."

He shook his head. "Well, I don't want to get tackled into the mud. I'll figure out a strategy."

We started the countdown and I stood in the mud pit, awaiting my plunge into the muck. The split second that we heard "GO!", Charlie started stripping his clothes off. In a matter of mere moments, the man went from dressed in a full Army uniform to buck naked, wearing nothing but his boots. It was the fastest I'd ever seen anyone undress. I guess he figured that if he was naked, the men would think twice about rolling around in the mud with him. But he thought wrong. They tackled him straight into that mud, undeterred, and began to wrestle mercilessly. My men ran straight for me as I had anticipated and soon the mud-pit was nothing but a dirty blend of arms, legs, elbows, and one man's privates.

When the wrestling finally came to a close, we waded out of the pit—covered head to toe with muck—and poured water over ourselves, trying to wash off as much mud as possible. And then in the wee hours of the morning, the whole group of tired, muddy, but happy men ate barbecue together, still poking fun at Charlie. We laughed uncontrollably as I recounted how every time I would get picked up and slammed down on the ground, I'd look up to see Charlie's penis just waving overhead.

That day was the beginning of the culture and closeness that Legion would be known for. We trained hard, pushed hard, and laughed even harder. I looked around that night, knowing that the peace would not last. These same men would have to face challenges that they couldn't imagine in the coming months. This camaraderie would be the bond that would pull them through.

In January of 2006, we caught wind that our unit would be up next to deploy, most likely in the fall. I did my best as temporary company commander to make sure that my men were ready, all the while expecting to meet my replacement any day. A June date was set for my men to attend one of the Army's large national training centers, which was required in preparation for deployment. I didn't expect to be a part of that training, as I assumed that I would be phased out of command by then. I had decided that when they found a replacement for me, I would turn in my Special Forces

Assessment and Selection packet in hopes of pursuing the opportunity of being a Green Beret. The desire to be a part of a special forces team had always been a dream of mine and it felt like the right time to chase it. The training that would be involved would also keep me in the US for at least a couple of years before deploying, which was a good thing now that I had a new baby on the way.

It was a day in early spring when my boss, the battalion commander, and his boss, Brigade Commander Colonel Roberts, called me into the office. I was expecting to hear the news that a new company commander was on the way and ready to replace me. Instead, they sat me down and told me that they had been watching me and were happy with the job I'd been doing as company commander. Then, they asked me to stay in command for the upcoming deployment. They told me that due to the fact that there had been so much change in leadership among the other units throughout the reflagging process, they liked the fact that me and my men knew each other well. We had been together in the same rough areas, braved combat, and built trust with each other during our previous deployment. They told me that they were pleased with the leadership I had exhibited thus far and they knew that with my experience in combat I'd be the right man for the job. The decision to say yes to such a huge opportunity was a no brainer, but it didn't come without sacrifices. Though I could pursue the path toward becoming a Green Beret later, I knew deep down that, by saying yes to this command, I was probably giving up the dream to become special forces for good. I also knew that I'd be saying goodbye to my newborn baby within a few short months of the birth. But even still, I was excited to stay with my men and see them through the deployment.

Crissy was supportive of my decision and was happy about the fact that we would be able to keep the house instead of selling it to move somewhere for training, which would have been the case had I pursued becoming a Green Beret. But she also understood that she would have to walk through much of the baby's first year alone, and this weighed heavily on her. This realization hit me as well, but my mindset had already undergone a severe shift as I prepared to step back into such a dangerous environment, this time as a company commander. As in the months leading up to my first deployment, the emotional space between Crissy and me widened again as I withdrew from everyone, trying to block out anything that would hinder my ability to effectively lead and serve in the coming months. The lives of dozens of men now rested squarely on my shoulders, and the weight of responsibility caused me to push anything I deemed a distraction out of the way. And that meant protecting myself against the emotion tied to leaving behind my wife and newborn baby. The task ahead would take every ounce of my heart, brain, and body, and I couldn't afford even a thought of anything else cluttering my mind. Crissy felt my withdrawal, and though we didn't talk about it much and we didn't fight, an all-too-familiar distance settled between us.

In early spring, I went with Crissy to a sonogram appointment to discover if we were having a boy or a girl. Unfortunately, the tiny human inside of her had other plans and was turned in such a way to prevent that all-important look between the legs to determine whether we'd be buying overalls and trucks or pink dresses and tiaras. Another sonogram was set for a later date, but I was already scheduled for a ten-day training out in the woods during that time. I was disappointed to miss the big moment, but there wasn't anything I could do. A few weeks later, I sat with 1SG Orlando Garcia up in a tower, conducting a gunnery exercise, overlooking my men on the ground who were cycling through runs on the range. My phone rang and it was Crissy. My heart leapt as she told me that I was having a son. I beamed with pride, picked up the radio, and shared the news with all the men. Whoops and hollers rang out as they celebrated that moment with me.

In June, while at the National Training Center in California, I was promoted to captain. My superiors conducted a small ceremony for me. As soon as it was over, I headed back out to train with my unit and braced myself for what would surely be next. A group of my men began to circle around me, and I inwardly groaned. *Here it comes,* I thought. They tackled me and beat the living crap out of me. It was tradition. They didn't punch me in the face or nose, but there were many strategic kicks and elbow jabs as we wrestled and tussled on the ground. I came out with a busted nose, a cut on my head, and the satisfying confidence that my men truly liked me. When you get promoted, the men jump you if they like you and they don't if they hate you. So, I nursed my scrapes and bruises with a smile.

Everyone was getting close and we had more than our fair share of laughs as we continued to train during those months. One morning, as I sat in my office, a quiet, unassuming young soldier named Brian Portwine came in to pour himself a hot cup of joe from the coffee pot. Now, this was no ordinary coffee pot. It had been with us all the way through the first deployment, it had braved Hurricane Katrina, and it had faithfully fueled countless tired soldiers with fresh coffee. It was every bit as much a part of Bravo company as the soldiers, and everyone knew it.

As Brian went to get his coffee, another soldier by the name of James Jeffers towered leisurely in the doorway. Jeffers was one of the scariest son-of-a-bitches you've ever met. He had endured more harrowing combat action than anyone and could probably kill a man with his bare hands and a spoon. And, as if his natural brute strength wasn't enough, the look on his face quickly informed you that he was not to be messed with. One could only hope to stay on his good side. This particular morning, Jeffers watched as young Brian quietly pulled out a mug and picked up the coffee pot to pour himself a fresh cup. But just as he did, the coffee pot slipped and crashed to the floor, shattering into hundreds of tiny pieces.

As soon as the sound of breaking glass subsided, the room went dead silent as we all stared at Brian. He looked back at us with wide eyes, knowing how sacred that broken item had been. He genuinely looked scared for his life. Jeffers broke the silence with an even voice that left no room for questioning: "Dude, start running. Because... You. Are. Dead."

Brian didn't hesitate to see if he was serious or not. He bolted out of the room with startling speed. We called him in a few hours later and solemnly informed him that, although Jeffers would not kill him, this coffee pot was part of the company and deserved a proper burial. He understood. He picked up every shard of glass, packed it away, and a few days later we gathered the men for the memorial service. We tasked Brian with officiating. Brian dug a grave, built a tombstone, and then stood on the steps beside the headquarters building and read aloud a eulogy that he had written in honor of the coffee pot. I don't remember what all he said, but the men laughed all through it, and he ended with this line: "You may have been made in China, but you were more American than any of us."

As the bond between the men grew, it wasn't uncommon for friendly brawls, wrestling matches, and general goofing off to erupt as soon as we broke formation at the end of the day. On one such day, I stood towards the back of the group next to Mike Krayer, my XO, taking in the sight before me. The men laughed and wrestled on the ground, rolling around in a display of health, strength, and friendly aggression. I watched them breathe the fresh air, blood pounding through their veins as they played, knowing all too well that in just a few short months that very pulse and breath could be taken by the enemy that we were about to face. I turned to Mike as we both watched the sight before us and said, "Embrace this and enjoy it. We have to prepare ourselves for the fact that this, this brotherhood and this bond, is what will make us great but is also what will make it that much harder when we lose someone. Our job won't be easy. We are the glue that has to hold these men together when all hell is breaking loose."

Those same thoughts ran through my head often as we prepared for what lay before us. And despite my efforts, I couldn't distance myself completely from the thought of what my own son could lose. But every time those feelings sprang up, I would consciously shut them off, not daring to let my emotions cloud my ability to effectively do my job.

On a Saturday in late July, I received a call in the middle of the night that something had happened to one of the men who had just recently joined our company. I rushed to the hospital, along with 1SG Orlando Garcia, and we found out that he had been in a car accident. We waited at the hospital through the night. As morning came, we received the news that he had passed away. I stayed there all day Sunday, trying to do what I could in the aftermath of his death, and then drove back home with a heavy heart. The very next night Crissy went into labor, two weeks before her due date, and my son was born. We named him Cole Adam Morris, in honor of Adam Malson, my brother and friend who had passed away while serving in Iraq. In the months prior to Cole's birth, I had contacted Adam's father, Ben, and asked permission to name my son in honor of his. I also contacted Adam's widow, Lindsey, and asked her permission as well. They both said yes. When Cole was born, I snapped a picture on my flip phone and sent it to just a handful of people, including Ben. I hoped that they would somehow find comfort in knowing that Adam's memory and legacy would carry on through the life of my son. I quickly received a response from everyone I sent the picture to, except Ben. I worried that perhaps the reality of their loss had set in or the picture had been too much or too soon. But two months later, I received this letter from Adam's father:

Dear Cole Adam Morris,

Recently your wonderful parents sent me an email

announcing the birth of you into this beautiful world.

Maybe one day you will be told a story of a brave

young man who fought for our country and Iraq's

freedom. The ending of the story is sad, but it's the

sacrifice that some have to pay in order to secure

freedom.

His wife, Lindsey, sets an example for all to follow.

She is a strong, brave, and dedicated young woman.

Lindsey misses her husband. She seems to keep moving

forward utilizing Adam's energy. Most people call it

love and I agree.

Be proud of your middle name. My wife and I selected

our son's given name because he was the first boy born

of the third USA generation Malson family. Fittingly,

his name is borrowed from the first man on earth.

My advice to you is to live a long and stellar life.

Listen to your parents.

Share time with the people in your life.

Study hard in school and try your best at anything you

set out to accomplish.

Be kind to all, but don't let anyone ever bully you,

your family members, or friends.

Welcome to the world of life.

Respectfully yours,

Ben and Debra Malson

That letter was by far the single greatest gift we were given with the arrival of Cole. I read it over through tears many times and tucked it away, waiting for the day that I would read it to Cole. I would tell him about a great soldier named Adam, the legacy that will live on through him, and what it takes to be a man in this world.

Our deployment date was set for October 26th. Just three days before our departure, I got another call in the middle of the night with a strained voice on the other end: "Sir, something has happened to one of the men. You've got to get up here." I gathered my things and immediately headed to the hospital, which was located about an hour and a half away. Upon arriving, I learned the devastating news that one of our best and brightest, a man named Joseph, had gone out to celebrate and party with a few friends and had suffered an alcohol-related incident. The doctor informed us that he was completely brain dead, but had not passed away yet. He lived just long enough for his family, who lived in Colorado, to make the fourteen-hour drive to say their goodbyes. The sadness in the waiting room was unbearable. There's nothing like facing a parent who is grieving the loss of their child, and as I looked into the eyes of Joseph's parents it killed me to think that it might not be the last time I'd have to do just that.

We conducted a memorial service for him the following day as we continued to make preparations to leave only two days later. I had come to grips with the fact that we might lose men while deployed, but it was an unsettling feeling to lose two men before we even left US soil. Perhaps these deaths should have registered as an omen of what was to come, bringing some premonition of darkness ahead. But we felt strong, unified by our familiarity and camaraderie. We were soldiers. We were friends. We were bonded brothers. We were Legion. What could this next deployment throw at us that we weren't prepared for?

Two days later, it was time to say goodbye and leave for Iraq. I didn't want the men to see me break down or cry so I walked Crissy and Cole outside to say our final words. For so many months I had suppressed all the feelings tied to what lay ahead and what would be left behind. Crissy and I walked to my truck, which would now be hers, and I held Cole close to me. When we got to the car I took the tiny bundle that was my three-month-old son and laid him in his carseat. I said my goodbyes to Crissy and then turned to say my final farewell to Cole. As I stared into the little face that so innocently looked back at me, all the walls around my emotions crumbled. I took him in, his peaceful breathing, his small features, his awaiting future. All I could think was, *What if I never see him again? What if this is the last time? What if he grows up without a father?* Very few things could take my breath, but as I stared at my baby boy that day, I could scarcely inhale under the weight of what could be lost.

When Crissy and Cole drove off, I started walking. Only a little time remained before I had to return to my men. With each step, my heart ached. I never wanted my son to question the love I had for him. I cherished him with everything in me. But I knew the task that lay ahead of me. I simply couldn't allow myself to feel this flood of emotion until I stepped back onto American soil again and held Cole in my arms. And so, just like that, I flipped the switch. I felt nothing. It was time to begin again.

Chapter 8

"There's a shadow just behind me, shrouding every step I take."—Tool, Sober

Iraq, November 2006

An odd sense of unsettling familiarity washed over me as I inhaled a lungful of Iraqi air once again. It felt like just yesterday that my boot touched the same sandy soil when I arrived in Iraq for the first time, young and eager to taste the flavors of combat. Much had changed since then. I had changed since then. This time, I was a father. This time, the responsibility to lead over a hundred men rested squarely on my shoulders. And this time, I understood the cost and sacrifice involved in fighting this war. The memory of Adam and the knowledge that he breathed his last breath in this very place lay fresh on my mind.

My unit wasted no time beginning the transition of relieving the existing unit, which had been stationed there for over a year. The customary transition process usually took two weeks. During the first week, the existing unit would ride in the driver's seat while the men from the new unit would ride as passengers, taking time to get to know the lay of the land, meet the locals, and learn from the men who had been there. The second week, it would switch, with the men from the new unit as the drivers and the outgoing men as the passengers.

My men sat patiently in their position as passengers that first week, watching and learning everything they could. On the second week, they eagerly jumped into the driver's seat while the outgoing men contentedly sat back as passengers, ready to finish their work and get on a plane to return home. A fresh sense of energy flowed through all of us as we grasped the baton being handed over. It was our turn. Our unit had a particular chemistry and connection that made us strong, and we knew it. We had trained hard for many months and it was time to put it all into practice. The outgoing men held their heads up high, knowing that they had completed their mission, and were now only days away from greatly anticipated embraces in the airport from wives, children, and parents.

The handover appeared to be going seamlessly. But on the final day of the transition period, I received a call. My heart sank as I learned the news that our engineer company, accompanied by the outgoing engineer company, had been hit by an explosive. One of our men and two of the men from the outgoing unit were killed. We had only been in country a little over a week and already we had lost one of our own. And though we didn't have the opportunity to know the two men from the outgoing unit well, it was still a sobering blow to realize that they had been killed while on the way back from their final mission, on their final day, only hours away from picking up their duffle bag and flying home. The news of these deaths hung ominously over us. It was as if the war felt compelled to remind us all that battle, and the casualties it brings with it, has no partiality and gives preference to no man. There were families who would be making dinner reservations and plans to do all the things they had waited a year to do with their loved ones, families who now would receive a phone call that would change everything forever.

As we began to settle in, rumors circulated of a video that had just been released. It was said to be a recording of an enemy sniper conducting hits on American soldiers. All of the men, myself included, couldn't help but pull up the video and press play, like the proverbial train wreck that you don't want to watch but can't look away from. A dark and haunting tune began, the backdrop to the real-life violence that now played before us. We all watched the screen in horror as fifty American soldiers were shot to death. When it ended, we walked away silent, a pit in our stomachs, reminded that all around us lurked the kind of evil that would take twisted pleasure in the slaying of American soldiers. No one said it, but we all thought it: "Am I going to be on a video like this?"

Not long after, we watched as President Bush addressed the United States, informing the American people of a new strategy that would be implemented in Iraq. He spoke of a surge of units, more than 20,000 men, that would be sent to flood the region. This increase of American forces would be dispatched in hopes that it would help to stabilize the area once and for all. The vast majority of the men, five brigades, would be sent to Baghdad. The surge brought with it more implications than just an increased number of men being added to our ranks. I was informed that part of this new strategic plan would involve decreasing the number of large bases that were set up in the region in conjunction with sending the men out into the local area to live among the people. I understood the logic behind the plan, but I also knew that our living conditions, which we had grown accustomed to, would change drastically as a result of this new strategy. I didn't look forward to informing my men about the change. We were also notified that our deployment had been extended by an additional three months. Now, instead of looking at a year away from our families, we were staring down a full fifteen months. For those of us who left in October, that meant that we would miss two holiday seasons with our families. It was a hard truth to accept, the fact that I would miss Cole's first two Thanksgivings and Christmases. We were off to a disheartening beginning.

We settled into FOB Rustamiyah, which was located east of the Tigris River. Previously, I'd been stationed on the west side of the Tigris River, patrolling Haifa Street and the area around it. Now I was placed just southeast of where I had been during my first deployment. Our unit was assigned a much larger area this time around, a region known as 9 Nisan, which we divided up, each company assuming responsibility for a particular sector. The area that Bravo company was assigned to required the farthest drive from FOB Rustamiyah and there were two routes to get there, Route Pluto and Route Predator. We were warned that these two roads were known for being heavily targeted by the enemy and for the prevalent use of IEDs and EFPs (Explosively Formed Projectiles). Though both were highly dangerous, the use of EFPs was a fairly new tactic and bore a particularly damaging threat to us. An IED is simply a bomb. It's dangerous and deadly to be sure, but straightforward. EFPs are different. To understand an EFP, imagine you have a paint can; now, picture taking the lid off and packing it with C4 explosives. Then, imagine taking copper plates and placing them on a press machine that indents them down and seals them on the lid. When the C4 blows, it takes that copper and turns it into a molten slug that can penetrate anything. With an EFP you're not getting a huge shrapnel-forming bomb like you would with an IED, which was often ineffective at penetrating our Bradleys. Instead, you get a projectile that can destroy anything it touches, including our heavily armored vehicles. The impact of an EFP also created a torrent of shrapnel, which only added to the threat that it posed. The knowledge that the route we would be driving every day was known for explosions of this nature left us feeling exposed and vulnerable as we ventured out onto the streets.

As the months went on, I realized how much had changed since the first deployment. The enemy was improvising and getting smarter in their tactics every day and had evolved greatly since I had last been there. During the first deployment, our opponent was embodied in figures running in the streets that we could chase. They had faces we could see. Now, it was as if we were fighting a ghost. When explosions would erupt, the ones pulling the trigger were always long gone by the time we could move to retaliate. The strategy behind the strikes was well thought out and it oftentimes left us baffled and frustrated. In another life, we wished we could talk face-to-face with those we fought and ask them how they were able to carry out particular hits without being caught. The creativity behind many of the attacks was brilliant in its own kind of sick way. Sometimes, they would take out the floor in the backseat of a car and load it with an IED. One man would drive to a curb, park, get out, and pretend to look under the hood while another would remove the fake floor and slide an EFP in place on the curb below. It was a perfect plan. They were masters at disguising EFPs to look like everyday items, cleverly making them take on the appearance of a curb or garbage in the trash piles, forming them into many shapes and sizes, all deadly.

We rapidly oriented ourselves to these new tactics and learned the lay of the land, adjusting to how different the elements of this fight would be from before. During the first deployment, we only went out on the streets when there was a clear mission before us to execute, such as conducting the Thunder Runs, searching a building, or pursuing a particular man. Now the mission was simply to patrol our sector twenty-four hours a day, as a means of establishing our presence with greater force in the area. I divided our company into smaller groups and tasked each one with patrolling a particular sector.

In the months that followed, our time was occupied primarily with doing six- to eight-hour patrols every day. We weren't kicking down doors, pulling triggers, or chasing insurgents down the street like we had before. Instead, we drove. A lot. This only made us a predictable, obvious target for the enemy to hit with explosives, and everyone knew it. It was a rather dispiriting time for the men and many adopted the sentiment that, without a particular mission in mind, there was no reason to rightly justify the risk of venturing out on the roads.

Despite all of that, I knew why it was valuable for American troops to be active and visible and I understood the importance of the mission we were given. This was a long game of establishing stability in the region, which was a worthy goal. But, in the short term, I knew that we weren't going to see many tangible wins. I tried to create a sense of purpose behind our patrols, focusing my men on tasks such as driving to a nearby school and patrolling the area around it or knocking on doors and meeting the locals. We adopted a sort of counterinsurgency model in our work, trying to establish trust and rapport with the community. But it was hard to get away from the fact that our long patrols gave ample opportunity to be targeted by the enemy.

The surroundings in our area were especially rough. I had seen the undesirable conditions of the shanty towns that stood behind the tall, new buildings that lined Haifa Street. But this was worse. Now, there were no large buildings to cover up or distract from the sights and smells that greeted us every time we went out. Raw sewage was prevalent and ran in thick streams on the side of the roads. The houses were crowded together, electrical wire wound through the streets, and puddles of mud lay everywhere. Every day we drove past what we called "Dead Cow Road," which was simply a place where the locals dumped the carcasses of dead cows, donkeys, and horses. The unimaginable stench of rotting flesh hung heavily in the humid air on that stretch of road. We joked that we were certainly safe in the area because even the terrorists and insurgents wouldn't brave that awful smell.

It wasn't long before I received the call that I had been dreading since my arrival, informing me that one of our Bradleys had been hit. My pulse raced as I waited to hear how bad it was or if anyone had been injured. Miraculously, everyone made it out alive. When they brought the Bradley back, we examined where it had been hit, awestruck by the chunk that the EFP had effortlessly taken out of the vehicle. Not long after, another EFP hit one of our Bradleys, exploding near the rear end. No casualties resulted, but one of our men, sitting in the back holding a plate of food and about to take his first bite, was hit in the head by the massive dent that the explosion made in the Bradley. He took it like a champ, looking up as soon as he was hit and saying, "Well shit, looks like I just lost all my dinner." We considered ourselves lucky, knowing that the explosions that Legion had experienced could have been worse.

I knew heading into this deployment that things would be tough, but the challenges we faced were much harder than expected. Though there was a particular exhaustion I felt in the first deployment from the highs and lows of heart-pounding combat we faced, this time I began to feel that I would choose that fight any day over the disheartening battle we now found ourselves in. When you go out on a raid, catch one of your opponents, place him in handcuffs, and bring him back to base for questioning, you have a tangible win. When you can see two figures running away from an explosion and you have a trigger you can pull that results in two less men being operational in the mission to threaten and terrorize others, you have a tangible win. But with the drastic increase in the masterful use of IEDs and EFPs, we had a faceless enemy. After the deafening sound of an explosion, only silence reigned. It was maddening. Seldom was there a visible target to aim towards; rarely could we engage the enemy in a way that resulted in a concrete, substantial victory that we could rally around and share the triumph of. This battle would primarily be fought by simply showing up every day and bringing our presence to the streets of this torn and hurting country.

As we fell into our daily routine, another understanding sank in: just how different being a company commander was from being a platoon leader. There were many decisions that had to be made as a company commander and some were truly hard. We hadn't been in country long when I was told that I had to give up one of my platoons to an entirely different unit that didn't have any Bradleys. All of my men had trained together for many months, we had bonded, we had prepared for this mission, we had become Legion. It was hard to imagine sending anyone away. But in the end, I selected First Platoon to leave, and that resulted in hard feelings and a wave of backlash from among the men. First Platoon was last to be filled out with men, making it the place we sent all those who joined later. In some ways, I think they saw themselves as misfits or outcasts because they were the last to become part of Legion and felt I sent them to the other unit for those reasons. But that wasn't the case. Among First Platoon were several NCOs (Non Commissioned Officers) that I had served with in the first deployment. They weren't the flashy, funny, command-the-room kind of fellows, but they were solid and steady and I knew they'd make a great attachment to their new unit. Additionally, First Platoon Leader Josh Norton was an incredible individual. He was an Abercrombie and Fitch model in his college days and didn't necessarily look the part of a hardcore military man. But I knew for a fact that he was a skilled leader and one badass SOB. He commanded instant respect from his men and peers alike. Josh knew his stuff backwards and forwards but wasn't arrogant. In my eyes, he was perfect for the task of joining arms with a new unit, and I knew they'd quickly see how lucky they were to have him and the other men. There were many mixed feelings from the men about my decision, and that fact weighed on me. I knew that it is not a leader's job to make everyone happy, nor to justify or explain each choice that must be made. Nevertheless, it wasn't easy.

The time came, as part of the new strategy accompanying the surge, for us to leave FOB Rustamiyah and find a place to live among the locals. Breaking the news to your men that they have to pack their things and leave their comfortable surroundings, equipped with internet and television, and move into a building with much less sophisticated living conditions is not an easy task. After searching around a bit, we finally found a location to set up base and settled in by mid-February. Electricity was shoddy at best and the rooms were nothing much to look at, but this was now Legion Base and we made the best of it. We were not alone in doing this, as men from every unit were faced with the same task of finding a place to live among the community. All units lived on a constant rotation of staying at makeshift headquarters for four to five days and then coming back to FOB Rustamiyah for a couple days to get clean, do laundry, and rest up a bit before going back out again.

We settled into our routine and did our best to meet the local people and build trust with them. They seemed fine with us living among them, and we coexisted quite peacefully. A local sheikh welcomed us upon moving in and then warned us that there was one place in the vicinity that we ought not go. He pulled out a map and pointed to a road leading to a particular area where "the bad guys are". We began collecting intel and learned that the region he spoke of was a rural area that the enemy was using as a distribution hub of sorts to bring in new men and create EFPs, IEDs, and rockets to be dispersed around Baghdad.

A few weeks later, we received another promising piece of intel from an informant that we had been working with. He vehemently promised that he had something that we needed to see. He drove with us, pointed out a location, and told us to search the area, vowing that we'd find items of interest there. We followed the lead and began to dig around the designated spot, which was the yard in front of a mosque. We dug for hours but didn't find anything.

The next day, while driving to our patrol base from the main base, we suddenly heard an ear-splitting explosion. The thunderous sound literally shook our vehicle. We didn't see the explosion, but knew it must have detonated nearby. Within minutes, we got word that members of the Iraqi Army had been attacked not far from our location. We immediately headed in their direction to offer support. When we drove up and surveyed the scene, there was no enemy in sight, so we ran to the Humvee that had obviously suffered a blow from an EFP. We didn't say it out loud, but we were all thinking the same thing: this EFP had been meant for us. This attack had been planned as retribution for the digging we had done the night before.

As I neared the wrecked Humvee, I gaped in disbelief as my eyes took in the damage that the explosion had caused. A six-inch hole now sat where heavy armored plating used to be. We peered inside the vehicle, and the gory scene that lay before us was dreadful. Bodies lay lifelessly in pools of blood around the vehicle, severed into pieces by the force of the explosion. Innards hung out of the fragmented figures, mixing with blood that had sprayed across the floor and walls of the Humvee. It was gruesome. That was the moment we all fully realized what an EFP could do to the human body.

Not long after, on the evening of March 14th, 2007, we acquired promising intel that could lead us to a particular man we'd been chasing for months who was responsible for running a great deal of weapons in the area. We had received information about him many times before, but the searches that followed had always led to a dead end. We hoped that this time would be different. We were given orders to pursue the tip and search for him and were informed that a platoon from Charlie Company was headed over to provide additional assistance. The platoon from Charlie Company would meet me and Second Platoon at Legion Patrol Base and accompany us on the mission. Third Platoon was at FOB Rustamiyah for their refit time and we left them to rest up. When everyone arrived, I promptly spoke with my men and the leaders from the additional platoon and we put together a plan for the search.

After that, we gathered our things and drove to the general area indicated by the intel, which was full of ramshackle homes thrown together. Houses were built with wood, or cement, or whatever they could find, and the roads were all dirt. Trenches ran with raw sewage. Wires dangled everywhere from people tapping into electricity. Without a doubt, it was a shady part of town to be working our way through. The sun had set and darkness surrounded us as we stepped out of our vehicles and began the arduous task of searching for the man that we had been pursuing for so long. This mission was a break from our usual days filled with long patrols, and we all longed for a palpable victory. We set a security perimeter so that no one could get in or out and then began the drawn-out process of knocking on door after door and inquiring after the man we sought. I took the role of overseeing the operation, instructing the men on where to go and what to do. For hours we continued to rap on each door and for hours we found nothing. We began to wonder if this search would result in us coming up empty-handed just like we had every other time.

We had also been ordered to take part in a joint mission with the Iraqi Army early the following morning. This mission was set to be photographed, making it important to our superiors that a large number of men made a showing that day. The photos would no doubt be vastly circulated throughout the US media, and the desire to show the American people what our efforts were accomplishing was strong. I understood that, but as the hours passed and we advanced further into the night, I sent word back to my superiors, alerting them of how long the mission was taking, and asked for my men to be relieved of the joint mission so they could get some much-needed sleep. My superiors said no. Another hour passed, and another. I radioed in our status and asked again for my men to be relieved. They still said no. I then asked if I could send just Third Platoon, who was still resting at FOB Rustamiyah. Still they would not relent.

We continued our search long into the night. Finally, a small group of men radioed in, saying that they thought they had him. I hurried to their location, accompanied by my interpreter, to verify his identity. When I arrived, the man they had in custody matched every picture we had of him and our informant confirmed that he was indeed the man we were looking for. We placed him in handcuffs, led him to the back of our vehicle, and secured him inside. We then conducted a thorough search of the house for any other intel that might be there, a process known as Sensitive Site Exploitation, taking another couple of hours. The early signs of sunrise were drawing near when we finally finished.

Chapter 9

"Only the dead have seen the end of war."—Plato

Iraq, March 15th 2007

As we began the process of loading everyone back into their respective vehicles, I once again sent word to my superiors, asking for relief from the joint mission that was now only a couple of hours away. They compromised slightly and instructed me to send just half of Second Platoon. The original plan was for Second Platoon to meet Third Platoon (who had been resting at FOB Rustamiyah) at Legion Patrol Base so that we could drive up together for the joint mission. But after the events of the night, we now had a prisoner in tow and it was our job to get him back to FOB Rustamiyah for questioning. Our engines roared to life as we started the trip back. But before we had gone more than a few yards, I called for everyone to stop. I jumped out of my seat and ordered Second Platoon to drive back to FOB Rustamiyah and drop the prisoner off without me. I then instructed half of them to come back to Legion Base to meet Third Platoon for the joint mission. My seat was now vacant and I ordered PFC James L. Arnold to take my place. I knew it would take a couple of hours to process the prisoner and I hoped that they would get at least a little sleep before they headed back out. I headed to Legion Base to prepare for the mission and catch a bit of sleep myself.

About an hour later, I finally laid my weary head down and closed my eyes. Sleep had just washed over my body when a voice at the doorway woke me up with a start. "Sir, we just got word that Second Platoon has been hit by an EFP." I was fully awake now. With the memory of that blood-spattered Humvee fresh in my mind, I jumped up quickly to face the man who had spoken, a sergeant from the headquarters platoon. "Is everyone okay?"

"Based on what we know, it looks like everyone is alright," he told me. Relief swelled within me.

But my relief didn't last long. Just as I laid back down to sleep, the sergeant's voice again jolted me awake. "Sir, a secondary explosion went off and people are hurt. It doesn't look good." I knew each of the men in Second Platoon well and the idea that any one of them could be hurt, or worse.... I ran to the radio and jumped on, trying to get an idea of what had happened and how bad the damage was. A chaotic symphony of screams and stress-riddled voices rang out over the radio. We caught word that there was at least one KIA. Upon hearing that, I radioed in, ordering that no names be mentioned until we could confirm who had died. Alpha Company's patrol base was very near to where the hit had happened, and upon hearing of the attack they hurried to provide assistance in the aftermath. The injured men were rushed to FOB Loyalty, our brigade base that was equipped with a good medical facility. I was informed that there were multiple KIAs. A pit lodged in my stomach and my mind turned sickeningly over and over, wondering who it might be.

As I scrambled to figure out exactly who was hurt and what had happened, I received a radio message from Charlie Erwin, now the XO for Alpha Company, and I knew immediately from the sound of his voice that the situation was worse than I had feared. He didn't use our typical call signs but instead addressed me by name. "Jeff, this is Charlie. I'm about to call you." My phone rang soon after and I held my breath to hear what followed. He proceeded to tell me the names of four men who died.

As more details came in, I learned that after the first explosion detonated six men had gotten out of their Humvees to assess the damage and were hit by a second explosion, an IED loaded with ball bearings. Many of the ball bearings were over 10 mm thick and tore through the men's bodies without mercy, killing four of them instantly: Staff Sergeant Terry Prater, Staff Sergeant Blake Harris, Sergeant Emerson Brand, and Private First Class James Arnold. The other two men, Sergeant Nicholas Lightner and Sergeant Ryan Green, were left severely injured. Specialist James Coon, who was a gunner in one of the Bradleys, jumped out and dashed to their aid. He was able to stabilize the two wounded men until reinforcements showed up on the scene.

In the hours that followed the attack, the other half of Second Platoon, who had been resting back at FOB Rustamiyah, was tasked with returning to our patrol base, gathering the personal belongings of those who died, and seeing to it that everything was properly shipped back to their families. Everyone walked around in a state of total shock and numbness. I stepped in and became something of a platoon leader for a few hours, trying to hold the men together as best I could. But there was no way to push out the storm of thoughts and feelings that brewed inside me. I grieved the loss of these great men. I felt anger towards the enemy that was responsible for their deaths. And pangs of guilt gripped me over the fact that I had stayed behind while the men went ahead. I couldn't get the memory of ordering PFC Arnold to take my seat out of my mind. All I could think was, *It should have been me. I should have been in that seat.*

The remaining hours of the day were a blur and arrived exhausted at FOB Rustamiyah that evening. As soon as I pulled up, I asked to see the bodies of those who had died. 1SG Orlando Garcia joined me and we walked to the makeshift morgue that was on site. It was nothing but a large container, something you might see on the back of an eighteen wheeler. We walked inside and pulled out each of the long rectangular boxes that held within them the lifeless bodies of the fallen men. I had seen dead bodies before, but this was different. I stared into the pale, unmoving faces of four men who had become friends and brothers to me— men I had cried with, rolled around in the mud with, trained with, and joked with. Flashes of their laughing faces and the sound of their voices swirled through my head as I tried to comprehend the fact that they were really gone. They would never laugh again, never kiss their wives again, never have Christmas with their parents again, never see their children grow up. In a split second, their lives were snuffed out on a lonely Iraqi street. It just seemed wrong, in every way.

No tears sprang to my eyes and no large wave of emotion erupted. I felt dazed, numb to the reality before me. I stood there, not moving a muscle. Orlando suddenly broke, collapsing onto my chest under the oppressive weight of emotion brought by this loss. I pulled his head against my chest and held him. As his sobs began, I felt a flash of gratitude that, for once, I could be his rock for a few moments. While his tears soaked my shirt, my own welled up and poured down my face. And so we stood in that large container, under the dark Iraqi sky, beside the four lifeless bodies of our friends, and released the emotion we normally held inside. We lost all track of time. Eventually, the tears stopped and a sort of deadened exhaustion settled over us. Orlando pulled away and I looked down to see blood stains covering my shirt. A glance at Orlando revealed he was suffering from a terrible nose bleed. He dried up what he could and we walked back towards the main building.

I made my way to my room and found a figure standing inside—an army reporter, SFC Kap Kim, who had been following our unit for a while, for the purpose of researching a paper he was writing on the war in Iraq. Just days before, he had noted to me that Legion wasn't like any company he'd spent time with. He had talked about the particular connection and camaraderie we shared and how special it was. He had accompanied us on the mission the night before and had driven back to base with Second Platoon as they dropped off the prisoner. As I walked into the room, he came near and embraced me, tears in his eyes. "I'm so sorry," he said. He told me that he had been scheduled to leave that evening but couldn't after he heard what happened. He said that he felt he had to stay and finish the story he was working on. I spoke with him for a few minutes before it occurred to me that I hadn't eaten in over twenty-four hours. The thought of food hadn't even crossed my mind.

I headed to the cafeteria and grabbed a tray. Word travels fast and everyone knew what had happened. After placing a few items on my tray, I noticed everyone was staring at me and avoiding me as I moved about the room. Each pair of eyes shifted to avoid contact. My mental fog parted for a moment of clarity, and I looked down at my clothes. The blood from 1SG Garcia's nose had dried in a large crimson stain across my shirt, and given the events of the day, an easy conclusion could be drawn about where the stain had come from. A man from another unit approached me and said, "Sir, why don't you sit here and I'll go and get you a fresh shirt." I thanked him and told him that I would take my food to my room so as not to draw more attention.

I went back to my room and time passed in a blur. A few hours later, a helicopter landed to take the bodies. Everyone gathered around and lined the walkway as the coffins were carried past and placed on the helicopter. We stood up straight and saluted as the bodies were loaded, then the helicopter roared to life and a burst of wind gusted over us as it ascended.

Our company was given a few days to recover, as was customary when a significant death takes place among a unit. Each person deals with grief and the aftermath of trauma in a different way. Some exercise and work out, some burst out in fits of anger, some talk, and some just sit numb and silent. I had a few necessary duties to ensure that the personal belongings of the deceased were properly cared for and sent back to their families. Waves of emotion ebbed and flowed throughout the days following. I called Crissy and when she answered the phone I broke down. "I'm okay," I said, and then poured out the whole story to her. I kept close tabs on the condition of SGT Lightner and SGT Green. We were all thankful that, amidst this loss, we had their lives to hold onto.

We visited SGT Lightner and SGT Green on the 16th. Green was unconscious, but it was reassuring to simply sit and hold his hand, feel his pulse beating, and watch the rise and fall of his chest with each breath. The hospital contacted his family and arranged a call, one of the nurses holding the phone up to his ear so he could hear the voice of his mom, Lynda Kagan. Lightner was wide awake, talking and laughing, and it was a relief to hear his voice. We snapped a few pictures as we gathered around his bed, joking and smiling. Through all of the trauma of the last forty-eight hours, these two men were the only silver lining we had to cling to. I wrote this letter to a small group of friends back home:

"Devastated. There is nothing else that I can say at this moment in my life. Yesterday, tragedy struck my company in the worst of ways. Four of my soldiers were Killed in Action and two more were seriously wounded.

SSG Terry Prater - KIA

- son, husband, and father of 2 children

SSG Blake Harris - KIA

- son, husband, and father of 1 child

SGT Emerson Brand - KIA

- son, engaged to be married upon redeployment

PFC James Arnold - KIA

- son

SGT Ryan Green - WIA

SGT Nicholas Lightner - WIA

You cannot begin to fathom the magnitude of this tragedy on my guys. In our world, you prepare yourself mentally that losses may occur—but not four in one day.

I had been with SSG Prater for many years and watched him grow in the ranks. Last deployment he was awarded the Silver Star for valorous deeds in combat—the nation's 3rd highest award for valor in combat. SSG Harris I have had for just under a year, yet we were extremely close for the role he played in my company as the fire support NCO. SGT Brand was with me for just over a year. The consummate professional. He was quiet, unassuming, and excelled in everything. PFC Arnold was with me for the last year and a half. At 20 years old, he was more of a man than most 40-year-old men.

SGT Green is my favorite in the company—has been since the first day I met him. Every unit in the Army needs a SGT Green. Full of energy, always running his mouth and talking crap to someone in a joking manner. You cannot be around

SGT Green and not have a smile on your face. SGT Green is now missing his right leg, has a shattered left arm that was barely saved, and a shattered left hip. He has many years of recovery ahead of him and most in his position would never walk again. SGT Green will—I promise you; and I will be there when he takes those first steps, whenever it may be.

SGT Lightner is one of my medics; 'Doc' as we called him. Despite massive internal injuries that almost took his life on the battlefield, he attempted to bandage himself up. Between falling in and out of consciousness due to the loss of blood he suffered, he did his job as the medic on the scene and provided care to the other soldiers. His efforts saved SGT Green's life.

Unfortunately, this is not new to me and my men over the last few years. However, it is not something you can ever get used to. I stood over their bodies, waiting for them to hop back up as usual and carry on joking around like we always do. As fate would have it, I was with each for the last few hours before their death. SSG Prater and I were joking back and forth about who really deserved the credit for the bad guy we had just captured on a raid, him or me. Of course it was him, but I would never just give in to him. I was making fun of SSG Harris for why every time he works out he rolls his sleeves up so everyone can see the tattoos on his massive biceps. SGT Brand was quiet as usual; headphones on, wearing his usual stare of intensity, waiting to go after another target. Arnold was Arnold. Still a young boy in his 6'6" frame making everything he does look easy. Arnold carried half the squad's gear on his back and never complained a bit.

I stood there knowing, but not willing to accept, that they will never get up.

The details behind the incident are irrelevant, but trust me that the guys did it right. Unfortunately, the enemy has a vote sometimes and this day he won. I write this in confidence to you all that you will not share any details behind this incident. Feel free to share this with others close to you, but in no way pass any of this on to any type of media outlet or personal blog site. You have never given me a reason not to confide in you before; now more than ever, continue to earn that trust. All families have been notified, but some of the details may not have been fully shared and they deserve your respect and privacy.

We shall overcome. We have before and we will again. But for now, I mourn. Unfortunately a few of you on this list can fully appreciate my pain. I don't know much right now except numbness and that four of my soldiers are dead, two seriously wounded, and there are six families whose lives will now never be the same; neither will mine.

Jeff"

On the 17th, we made our way back to our patrol base and arrived carrying the emptiness left by those who were no longer with us. We were told that the memorial for the four men would be held on the 20th. We went out on patrols again, trying to get back into our routine. I led the missions, knowing how hard it was for the men to be back on the streets just days after such a traumatic event. It was important that there be no uncalled-for retaliation from our company. We kept the first missions simple, just venturing out into the area and driving around a little bit. A distinct heaviness hung in the air that none of us could shake. Even still, we all found a sense of hope and comfort in the fact that two of our men had survived the attack and that one of our own, Coon, had been instrumental in saving their lives.

As we went out on patrol for the second time since the men had died, some fragment of normalcy began to settle in. It was the 18th. While rumbling down the streets I received a call, informing me that SGT Green had just died from the injuries he suffered. I felt like I had been kicked in the gut. I didn't want to break the devastating news to the men while we were out, so I instructed everyone to quickly finish up and return to base. Once we were back, I gathered everyone and announced the news. As the words left my mouth the reactions were instantaneous. SGT Green had been the life of the company, dearly known and loved by everyone, and the thought that he was now gone was almost too much to bear. Now the upcoming memorial would be for five of our men.

We conducted the memorial on the 20th and emotions flooded out readily as many men, including myself, stood and spoke about the greatness of those we had lost. It wasn't hard to find things to say about each of the five men. Each man was unique, but they were all incredible individuals and were deeply loved by every one of us.

We made our way back to the barracks at FOB Rustamiyah and found ourselves gathering together. There was comfort in being with one another, some reminder that though we were wounded and torn we were still Legion and we still had each other. We cried a little bit more and then began to tell stories and laugh. Anyone who has experienced the death of someone close understands the healing power of laughter in the process of grief. The memorial provided us with a small sense of closure, and it was time to take the first step in moving forward as a company and getting back to the mission we still had before us. So we rallied around SGT Lightner, the only remaining survivor, and Coon, who had saved him, as a source of hope as we looked toward the future. SGT Lightner was being medically evacuated at the time for further care in the states, but his condition was stable. We received an update that he was doing well and that brought us all immense joy.

The next day, on the 21st of March, we drove back to Legion Base and once again tried to resume our normal routine. As we went out on patrol, my phone rang and my heart sank once again as I learned that SGT Lightner hadn't made it back to the states. He had died, due to his injuries, on the way to a US hospital. We had barely gathered enough strength to stand up again after the repeated blows we had been dealt, and this news hit our weakened nerves with a crushing impact. We conducted yet another memorial, for SGT Lightner, days later.

To lose six men in a matter of days is difficult, but their personalities and identities within our company made it absolutely devastating. We all felt exhausted and dazed. It felt as if every time the fresh wound of grief began to form a scar of closure another knife of loss plunged into the scab and burst it wide open, causing our hearts to bleed again. But even still, we knew that we had to continue with the duty and mission at hand.

A few weeks later, a couple of my men informed me privately that SPC Coon was struggling in the aftermath of the whole ordeal, replaying the events and feeling that somehow he could have done more for SGT Lightner and SGT Green. He was beating himself up for what happened, being eaten away by the guilt of wondering if he could have done more to save them. All the while, he had no idea that we were putting him in for a Bronze Star with Valor for jumping out when no one else did and risking his life to save two of our men. I hated to think of him being hard on himself when he should have been proud.

I called Coon into my room at FOB Rustamiyah a few nights later, on April 3rd, a time when I knew we'd have a chance to talk. He walked in, six feet and five inches of muscle. Coon was known for always being happy-go-lucky, goofy, flamboyant, and the life of the party; but as he entered my room that evening, there was a distinct soberness about him. When I met his eyes I could see the hollowness and pain he was holding. I told him to sit, asked a few questions, and then simply listened, allowing him to just talk. After he did, I met his eyes and said, "Look man, I know you feel down right now. I know you feel like you could have done more, but you couldn't have. No one could have done more and few would have even done what you did for those two men. You are only twenty-four years old, but you've accomplished more in the six months since you've been here than most people will accomplish in their entire lives. There are two families that got to have one more moment with their boy, because of you. SGT Lightner's family got to talk to him one last time, because of you. And even though he was unconscious, we got to put the phone to SGT Green's ears and his family got to say goodbye before he breathed his last breath, because of you. None of that would have happened if it weren't for what you did. Don't you dare feel guilty or discouraged. You walk around with your head held high for the rest of your life, because what you've done is pretty damn remarkable." The look in his eyes shifted just enough to show that my words had landed somewhere inside him. He simply said, "Thank you, sir."

The next day, on April 4th, I was back at Legion Base when a shot rang out. It sounded as if it came from across the river. Hearing a gun go off wasn't all that uncommon, so I didn't think much of it. Then the radio came to life. It was SGT Chris Hulsey. Chris was a rock. Nothing rattled him, nothing phased him, but when I answered the radio that day, his frantic tone scared me. "We're headed in and we need you to call ahead for a MEDEVAC."

"Who is it?" I asked.

"It's Coon. He's hurt. He's hurt real bad." I asked what the injury was so I could call it in and he told me that it was a head wound, from a sniper. By the sound of his voice, and given the nature of the wound, I knew that the situation was dire.

I found out later that Coon had been out on patrol with a handful of Bradleys and a few Humvees. They pulled up into a small area when a group of kids gathered around his Humvee, throwing candy and crowding in close to the vehicle. He had raised up to try and help move the group away from the Humvee, knowing the danger it could pose to have them so near. But when he stood up and leaned over the edge of the vehicle from his center position, a gunshot sounded. Everyone heard it, but no one knew where it came from. A sniper had fired and the shot hit Coon squarely in the head.

We were set up with a small medical aid station at Legion Base, and the men who had been on the scene headed our way with Coon. It just so happened that we also had the battalion doctor on site. I called for a helicopter and then gathered a few of the senior men, asking them to assist me in helping once Coon arrived. When the Humvee pulled in I ordered the rest of the men away from the scene, aware that what we were about to see wouldn't be good. Coon had been the hero that we had all been holding onto through this storm of grief, and seeing him in rough shape would break the spirits of those who witnessed him in that condition. The handful of senior men I had gathered ran with me to help transport Coon into the aid station as soon as the vehicle stopped outside. I told Chris, "Collect your men and leave as fast as you can so they don't have to see Coon like this."

One of the men accompanying me grabbed Coon's left leg, another grabbed the right, and I positioned myself to support his head. As we pulled him out of the Humvee, I looked down to see the makeshift bandage around his head sliding off. As it did, a blood-curdling, guttural noise erupted from his throat, and the utter pain and desperation it carried shook me to my core. It was a horrific sound that the human body should never make. His head rested on my forearm, and as the bandage slid off I could see the gaping wound caused by the large chunk taken from his head. His blood ran down my arm along with fragments of his brain. As soon as we got him to the aid station the doctor worked to stabilize his condition. Blood poured liberally out of the wound and spilled onto the floor. I grabbed towels and stooped to my hands and knees, trying to mop up the puddles so that no one would slip while trying to save him. Coon's desperate cries filled the room, a sound I would never forget.

When the helicopter landed we transported him rapidly to it. By that time he was unconscious. The other men and I met eyes, but we did not want to acknowledge what we all knew. Coon wasn't going to make it.

Everything was abruptly quiet. I watched as a few men began to clean the Humvee, mopping up a mixture of blood and bodily pieces that had spilled onto the floor during the transport. In a daze, I looked down at myself. What a bloody mess I was. It still remained to update the men on what was going on and I didn't want them to see me like this. I walked back to the bathroom near my room and shut the door. In a state of numbness, moving almost mechanically, I calmly removed from my arms the bloody fragments that had poured out of Coon's head wound. The mirror showed a crimson smear of his blood on my face, so I turned on the faucet, let the water pour into the sink, and then plunged my hands in. I splashed my face until it was wet and then dabbed soap onto my hand and began to lather it onto my cheeks. Suddenly, a burning sensation spread across my face. I leaned toward the mirror, coming eye to eye with my reflection, and saw a line of torn skin that ran beside my nose and up to my ear. As my frayed mind searched for an explanation, I became aware of the same burning sensation in my hands. It didn't make sense, and it was hard to think in the fog that hung heavily over me. And then a moment of clarity arrived, bringing with it a dreadful truth. As I studied my hands, I could see small chunks of sharp skull from Coon's head lodged into my skin. With a sickening feeling, I registered that the cuts on my face were caused by those very shards. The horror of the situation pierced through me, like nothing I had ever felt before. I didn't move a muscle for several minutes until the thought of my waiting men jolted me from my state of shock. As if in a dream, I finished cleaning myself and then walked out of the bathroom to address the men.

I received a call a few hours later, confirming what I already knew. Coon had died. I informed my men, whose faces reflected the brokenness I felt. After that, I headed back to FOB Rustamiyah to attend to a few necessary duties. Once completed, I went up to my room and sat down, holding my phone. I dialed the number of Jason Tucker, a friend of mine from back in the states. Jason was a quiet, solid, and steady sort of guy. He wasn't involved in the military but we still had a lot in common. We met through a mutual acquaintance, and both being huge Florida State fans, we bonded quickly and went to many games together throughout the years. Before I left for deployment I had given Jason a letter to hold onto in the event that I didn't make it back. I asked him to attend to my funeral arrangements and to be the primary male figure in Cole's life should the unthinkable happen. I had never called him from Iraq before, but on this particular night, I needed a friend.

The phone rang and he answered. "Hey, it's Jeff," I said.

"Are you okay?"

"No," I said. "I am, but I'm not. Look, I'm going to tell you something, and when I'm done, I don't want you to say anything. I don't want you to say I'm sorry, I don't want you to ask if I'm okay, and I don't want you to ask if there's anything you can do for me. I just want you to act like I never said it and never bring this conversation up again. I have something that I have to say out loud, because if I don't, I think it's going to mess me up pretty bad."

"Okay," he said. "Go."

I sat on my bed, and through the phone I told him everything that had taken place in the last few hours. When I was done, we sat in silence for a couple of minutes, the space between us heavy with the magnitude of the horrible events I had just shared an account of. There were no words that would heal or comfort or mend how broken I felt inside. In that moment, I couldn't bear to hear another human being even acknowledge the horrors I had spoken of. After a little while, his voice broke the silence. "Well man, it looks like Weatherford is going to be our quarterback next year. I'll keep you up to date, and if I hear anything I'll shoot you an email. Until then, Go Noles!" That was how we always ended our conversations. I said goodbye and hung up with appreciation for his response.

It would be a long time before I breathed a word to anybody else about what happened that day.

Chapter 10

"Beware that, when fighting monsters, you yourself do not become a monster... for when you gaze long into the abyss. The abyss gazes also into you."
—*Friedrich Nietzsche*

Iraq, April 2007

Rage. Unimaginable rage. It was all I felt in the weeks that followed Coon's death as I emerged from the daze of shock that had initially encompassed me after that day of horror. This rage burned with a volcanic heat as I mechanically continued to fulfill my daily duties. Feelings of sadness accompanied this fury, but sadness is gray and bleak, and the molten power of rage all but drowns it out. I hid my anger with effort, not allowing even a small eruption of what boiled beneath the surface.

I wouldn't dare let my inner turmoil be seen by my men, nor the hate I felt toward the enemy, nor my feelings of guilt from wondering if I could have done more as a leader to prevent the seven lives that had been taken, nor the thoughts I wrestled with as to whether this mission was worth the sacrifice of good men. I knew I had other good men counting on me to lead and to be strong. So I barricaded my feelings, rendering them undetectable from the outside. A few tears escaped my walls at Coon's memorial, but other than that occasion, I willed myself to never let the men see me cry. I continued to lead and push forward with the mission at hand, appearing undaunted to those around me. And yet at the end of the day, when no one was around, I would often close my door, sink onto my bed, and give freedom to the pent-up emotions that clawed and screamed to be released. In those moments, I would weep. But the tears that fell were not mournful, they were drops of fire and rage.

In war, there is no pause, no respite given to grieving soldiers, and IEDs and EFPs continued to explode frequently while we conducted patrols in the area. Our company suffered several more injuries as a result of the constant attacks, but in comparison to the deaths we had just witnessed, we considered ourselves lucky. But not everyone was so fortunate. A medic from one of our sister companies was killed during that time, a man who was very close friends with our medic. My heart sank when I received the news, knowing I had a tough conversation ahead of me. Bearing the responsibility of informing your men of the death of a fellow soldier is one of the hardest parts of being a commander. No one wants to put an arm around a young man and deliver the news that he'll never see his best friend again. And I was having these conversations far too often.

After the deaths of so many of my men it also fell to me to make the heartbreaking phone calls to the families of those who had died. Over the phone always came one inevitable question: "Did my boy die a hero? Did he die making a difference?" Without pause, I would always answer, "Yes, he did. He did his duty and made us proud. He made a difference and we're all better for it." And yet, so often as I said these words, a crushing weight of guilt settled over me. I strained to reconcile many aspects of the deaths I had witnessed over the past months, both the gruesome details and the knowledge that most of them died while completing a seemingly insignificant task. I bore the burden of knowing that there were children who would never see their daddy again, there were mothers who would never again hug their son, and there were wives who had become widows, simply because these soldiers were ordered to drive down a street on patrol. I never spoke these things to the moms or the wives. Instead, I told the families of their bravery, and the men were brave. I told the families of their heroism, and they were heroes. I said that the men died making a difference, and in the grand scheme of things, they did. However, I couldn't help feeling that I was telling a lie each time I answered their questions and made these statements. Too many of these deaths felt so pointless, so needless. And that thought cruelly burrowed deep inside me, only fueling my rage.

In April I received word that another one of my men, Scout Platoon Leader Josh Mantz, was wounded while providing backup to another unit under RPG fire. As he did so, a sniper fired, instantly killing the man beside him, Staff Sergeant Marlon Harper. The bullet ricocheted off of Marlon and hit Josh in the femoral artery. Blood poured out of the wound, and everyone around knew that the chances of his survival were slim. Although the medics did an incredible job caring for him and kept him alive, Josh fell into a short coma, and due to the excessive blood loss it was doubtful that he would ever come out of it. Knowing that a stud like Josh had been taken down was just another blow. He was strong, smart, and capable in every way, and it troubled us even more to know that an incredible man like him had been hit. Miraculously, Josh woke up and made a full recovery. He returned to duty just a few months later. I was thankful for the outcome, but sobered by yet another close call.

March had been bloody, and April was shaping up to be no different. There was no time to collect one's thoughts or gather one's composure after each attack, as the count of injuries and deaths continued to rise. I no longer attempted to go through the proper steps of emotionally processing each heartbreaking event. Instead, I switched into survival mode and simply plowed ahead, forcing myself to put one foot in front of the other and maintain a strong front for my men.

During that time, Josh Norton, who had previously been Legion's First Platoon Leader, took over as the Executive Officer in Alpha Company, our sister infantry company. While out on patrol, one of Alpha Company's Bradleys was hit by an IED. It immediately exploded into flames. Although injured, everyone jumped out of the vehicle, choking and unable to breathe, and ran to safety as a group. They soon realized that the driver was still inside, knocked unconscious, and left lying there as the vehicle continued to burn. Gunfire sounded from across the street, targeting the injured men. When Legion got the call, informing us of what was happening, two of our tanks simply responded with, "We'll be right there." They gunned their engines with no thought of the dangerous stretch of road ahead, one that was often riddled with explosives, and sped towards the scene. Upon arriving, the tanks were able to provide protection to the injured men from the shots being fired at them.

I heard Josh's voice over the radio from the patrol base, calm but strained with stress as he gave orders to his men while the situation continued to unfold. It's a tough job to lead with clarity within the chaos of bullets and injuries. But I was proud as I listened to him put his many months of training into action, directing his men and trying to figure out a way to save the unconscious driver who was still inside. The injured men managed to open the door of the Bradley, but couldn't pull him out. The flow of oxygen from opening the door gave fresh fuel to the fire. Soon the vehicle was engulfed in flames. Josh stayed strong and maintained his composure, but it was an impossible situation. Despite everyone's best attempts, no one could pull the driver out of the burning vehicle, and the state of the injured men was growing worse by the minute. They needed immediate medical attention. Josh gave the order for the injured men to evacuate and leave the driver behind, knowing that nothing could be done for him. As the men radioed back, we could hear their cries. Cries of pain and agony from their injuries. And screams of horror as they helplessly witnessed their friend and brother burning to death.

Situations such as these were taking a toll on the men. I did my best to hold it together, but the swell of turmoil inside was growing ever stronger. One day, a young private approached, asking if he could speak with me one-on-one. It is unusual for a private to directly ask for a personal meeting with the company commander. Typically, these types of requests are relayed all the way up through the chain of command, so I knew it must be important. I invited him in and closed the door. As we sat, I asked what was on his mind. He paused for a moment and then said, "Well sir, I'm struggling. I know I haven't been a part of this unit as long as some of the other guys, but I still hurt from all of the deaths that have taken place. I hurt for the way it's tearing up my brothers. It's hard, you know? I guess what I'm saying is... how do you do it, sir? You get up in front of the men and you talk strong and stand firm, reminding us that we have a job to do and rallying us to go and do it. Where do you pull the strength from?"

I thought for a moment before responding. "Look, just because you see me up there doesn't mean I don't have my own struggles. But we have a job to do here and we all have to find something inside of us that we can draw strength from. That 'thing' will be different for each man. You have to find it for yourself, and when you do, hold onto it. It will become your rock."

He nodded. "I'm so glad to hear you say that, sir. My rock is Jesus Christ. I pray every night for safety and protection, and I know He is going to take me back home to see my wife and children."

I should have nodded and encouraged him to hold onto that hope that he had inside. But in that moment, my own pain and shattered outlook temporarily surfaced. "Well man, that's great," I said. "But let me give you a little bit of advice. I know SSG Prater and SSG Harris both prayed together every night for the same thing, and look where they are at right now."

The young private met my eyes as the words fell out of my mouth and I saw a look of total deflation spread over his face. I had just told him to find something within that would bring him hope, I told him to hold onto it. But then, when he dared to show me the thing he clung to for assurance, I had taken it away from him. It wasn't that I didn't believe in God. But after seeing what happened to so many good men, it felt naïve to trust that a prayer would change everything. My intention wasn't to rob him of his trust and belief; I told myself that I was providing him with perspective, a reality check of sorts. However, I momentarily let my own unresolved pain snatch away a young soldier's hope. And when I registered the defeat in his eyes, I knew that speaking those words would forever be one of my greatest regrets.

My internal torrent of rage and grief continued to swell, but I did my best to be the leader that I knew the men needed during that difficult time. Not only were we dealing with the effects of deaths in our unit, but we were also forced to cope with the continual barrage of explosive attacks. At one point, so many of our Bradleys were destroyed that we couldn't even go out on patrol. None of us felt safe. Each day we awoke knowing that we might not make it back that night, a sobering realization which many soldiers throughout time have experienced. But what made this situation particularly demoralizing was the fact that we warred against a faceless enemy. We seldom had the opportunity to directly engage the evil that we came to destroy. Our days were spent patrolling the local streets, hoping that we wouldn't be hit. We all told ourselves that we were part of a greater good, and in many ways we believed that to be true. But it's hard to watch the blood of friends and brothers be spilled, all because you continue to drive down the same dangerous roads day after day.

In May, my time as company commander came to a close and my position was taken over by a man named Ron Sprang. I had known this day was approaching for a while—it was expected that I would give over command partway through the deployment. Even so, it's never easy to release a position of leadership. I knew my men well, and after all we had been through a large part of me wanted to stay and see them through the rest of the deployment. But another piece of me knew that having someone in command who was removed from the trauma and grief of the past few months would be a good thing. Upon meeting Ron, it was immediately apparent that my men would be in good hands. He was just what they needed and arrived at just the right time. The fact that it was only May meant that our company was staring down seven more months of deployment, and having a leader with fresh perspective would help to carry the company through the remainder of our time.

After everything that had happened, my superiors initially didn't feel that it was fair to Captain Sprang to have me around after the change in command took place. I knew all the men well, and we were so tightly connected that it would have been easy for them to come to me with questions and concerns rather than their new leader. I hated the idea of relocating. Though I understood the logic behind it, I disliked the thought of leaving my hurting unit. At the last minute, my superiors made the decision to let me stay and work in the S-3 shop, which handled operations. That way, I could be in close proximity and remain available to the men since they had been through so much. I took the role of Assistant Operations Officer, overseeing the team who manned the radios. In the event that someone was hit, it would be my job to coordinate and mobilize men to provide backup or assistance. Though I had the chance to help plan missions and operations, it was a definite change in pace from being company commander. It was my first "desk job" of sorts in the military, and though I learned a lot through the process, it was a difficult shift to make. The mundane cadence of my days caused the rage in me to turn to something worse: total and complete numbness. As the weeks passed, I completed my daily duties almost robotically, feeling a vast sea of nothingness inside. The total desensitization of my internal world was almost more unnerving than the blazing rage I had experienced before. I had no means for making myself feel again, and I began to wonder if I ever would.

On June 3rd, as I was working out at the gym at FOB Rustamiyah, my former XO, Luther Vallette, came into the room with an expression on his face that I had grown far too accustomed to within the past few months. Something was wrong. "Bravo Company just got hit, Jeff. You better come quick." I stood to follow him, bracing myself. We soon received word through the radio that there was a confirmed KIA, but we didn't know who it was. We waited. And waited. Finally the call came in, informing us that it was SGT Caleb Christopher who had been killed. Caleb was a great man— mature, professional, intense, the kind who always got the job done. I knew that he was just a couple of weeks away from going home on leave and was engaged to be married upon his return in January. Another death. Another good man gone too soon. There were no words anymore, no silver lining to hold onto. Our hearts could no longer be shattered, they simply remained broken.

I went home on leave in July. I had requested for my time off to be in coordination with my son's first birthday. My superiors were accommodating and agreed, allowing me to return home in time. I had already missed Cole's first holidays and knew I would miss his second ones as well, so I savored the chance to share this milestone with him. When I arrived, a wave of shock ran through me at the sight of him. He had grown since the last time I saw him, lying in his infant car seat in the back of my truck as I said goodbye. I pushed away thoughts of how much he would grow in the remainder of my deployment.

One of the highlights of my time off was celebrating Cole's birthday. We had some friends over for a party, and we all watched Cole go to town on a smash cake. I've still got a coffee mug with a picture of that happy little boy covered in blue and white icing. The other highlight was a very different sort—getting a tattoo in memory of the eight men from Legion who had died. I thought of each of them as the needle pressed into my skin, knowing that this ink would mark their memory forever. As for the tattoo, I decided on a Roman Gladiator/Spartan theme. On the image there was a shield with the words "I Tan I Epi Tas" on it. Translated, it read, "with it or on it." This was the parting phrase that Spartan mothers would say to their sons as they went off to battle: "Carry this shield home with you, with it or on it." And so I had the initials of the fallen eight engraved on the outer edge of the shield, symbolizing that they had come home "on it."

My leave passed by quickly. I spent as much time as possible with Cole, striving not to think about the fact that he likely wouldn't remember me when I came home. Crissy did a good job of showing him pictures of me while I was gone, but photographs weren't the same as getting to share face to face time with him during his first year of growing up. I hated the reality that I was missing so much of his life.

After getting dinner with friends in Austin one night, Crissy and I loaded Cole in his carseat and hopped in our vehicle to head for home. We had a forty-five minute drive ahead of us to the suburb where we lived. I started the car and began driving. The minutes ticked away, the music on the radio the only sound as we drove under the night sky. We weren't angry. We weren't upset. We were just silent. As if we didn't know where to start.

As we neared home, I broke into the quietness. "When I get back, we're going to have to completely start over. We have nothing in common anymore. And I know that is primarily because of me." I stared ahead, waiting for her response.

She thought for a moment and then nodded. "I know. You're right. I just don't know what to say to you after all you've been through."

I understood. We loved each other, we even enjoyed each other's company, but it was hard to know where to begin intertwining the strands of our life together after spending so much time apart. There were experiences I had been through and things I had seen that had changed me. It created a distance between us that neither of us knew how to close.

All too soon, I kissed Cole and Crissy goodbye and returned to Iraq for the second part of my deployment. My days consisted of working at the S-3 shop and working out in the gym like a madman. I pushed myself hard, the burning lungs and aching legs somehow a welcome feeling in my world of numbness. The severe workouts served as an outlet of sorts for all that was pent up inside of me, things that I couldn't even acknowledge or give voice to anymore. Those long hours in the gym resulted in me being physically stronger than ever before.

I received a phone call from Crissy one day, not long after returning, and her tone of voice made it clear she had something she needed to say. "I've been thinking a lot about what you said that night in the car," she said. "I think it's best that we go ahead and start planning for how life is going to be when you get back." I knew what she meant and that this conversation was most likely the beginning of the end of our relationship. And though I felt upset in some ways, in other ways I remained unfazed. Life had become almost transactional. Black and white. Yes or no. In or out. There was no more gray in my mind, no more strength for convincing or changing minds.

My internal world was a vast space of emptiness. I remained darkly consistent and unchanged by any situation thrown in my direction. Nothing excited me or made me particularly happy. Nothing crushed me or made me sad. No unvoiced screams of pain or words of anger anymore, only cold silence inside. I had become weathered and worn down, unfeeling, untouchable. The only thing that brought a sense of love and joy to my lifeless heart was thoughts of Cole. And I held on dearly to the hope of holding him again.

A few weeks later, we received the news that a young soldier who had only recently joined us was on one of his first patrols when his Humvee was hit by an IED. The blast didn't directly wound anyone, but it caused the Humvee to roll over, trapping the young man in the vehicle and in a trench of thick sewage that ran beside the street. He didn't die from an explosion, or wounds from a sniper round. No, he simply drowned. The grotesque image of a bright, youthful boy, not even twenty years old yet, inhaling lungfuls of feces and urine as he suffocated sickened us all to the core. How do you tell a mother that her son spent his last moments alive swallowing sewage beside a dusty road in a dirty shanty town? How do you fit that piece into the grand scheme of believing that all these deaths were serving some ultimate purpose, some greater good? How do you carry on as usual after the knowledge of something so unspeakable?

I sat in the S-3 shop not long after, observing the feed from the JLens that we had positioned in the sky, watching as another Humvee drove toward FOB Rustamiyah. As it approached the gate, I watched in horror as the vehicle exploded before my eyes. A team ran to the scene immediately and confirmed yet another KIA. That night, one of the men came in and sat down, a despondent look on his face. "Well guys, I have to tell you something that will ruin your day, probably your week, hell... your year." He went on to inform us that the man who had been killed that afternoon was at his patrol base when he heard the news that his wife had just given birth back in the states. A special convoy was commissioned to get him and bring him back to FOB Rustamiyah so that he could use the video conferencing room to see his wife and meet his new baby. But on the way, right outside of the gate, just minutes away from meeting his child, he was killed.

We all sat back in silence, thinking of the woman who went through the pains of childbirth alone, who stayed strong to make her husband proud, who sat up straight in the hospital bed and looked expectantly toward the screen, holding a tiny package in her arms, whispering into the baby's ear that it wouldn't be long before he would meet Daddy. We all pictured the eager father, rushing and smiling with the realization that he was about to see his beautiful wife and baby. And we thought of the smoking Humvee and blood-spattered man who would now never see his child grow up.

There are always casualties in battle. But sometimes war creates scenarios that even the most hideous and sinister of minds could not imagine. It was as if some great evil wished to remind us that our lives, hopes, and dreams held no value... that sons could be tossed to the edge of the road to die in bodily waste, that fathers could be executed just moments before meeting their child, that nothing any man held dear was sacred. We each felt vulnerable, knowing that not one of us was protected against the clutches of death. We wrestled to believe that what we were doing was worth this constant loss of life. We struggled to find within us the fire that had driven us to stand up and become part of this mission in the first place. The American people had the luxury of seeing the war as a whole, viewing the apparent good and advancement that were taking place, as though soldiers were pieces in a board game. We, with each step forward, had to witness the bloody deaths of dear friends, and hear the screams of young men burning to death, and watch lives obliterated before our eyes. And we struggled to find the purpose for it all.

During that time, we also witnessed the effects of the civil conflict between the locals, primarily between the Sunnis and Shias. One day we came upon the body of a man who had been tortured and killed by one of his own countrymen. The body was a gruesome sight to behold. Bloody holes covered him, the result of slow and meticulous torture with a drill bit. The bit had been inserted into the flesh of his eyes, his ears, his penis. Looking at the aftermath of such unspeakable acts is something that changes you. You can never unsee those things. What would cause a person to inflict that kind of torment on another human being? There are many men who have taken the life of another in rage or revenge. But this was so personal, so methodical, so hideously creative, it caused me to wonder how anyone could be capable of this act. Though sickened and repelled, the sheer will to execute this kind of horror on another person is something I almost admired. This was a display of utter human strength, demonstrated in the most depraved of ways. What would it look like for someone to wield that same kind of power, force, and resolve but choose to use it for good?

The surge had swelled to full capacity by the time summer arrived. The attacks remained constant, and the injuries and death count continued to rise. But the tide shifted drastically when Shiite cleric Muqtada al-Sadr called for an end to the ongoing violence and clashes between the government and his Mahdi Army militia. After this statement was made public, the attacks diminished greatly. They didn't come to a complete halt, but they were few and far between, which made the last months of deployment very slow and quiet.

This lull gave me time to ponder what the next chapter of my life was going to look like. For so long, all I could see was my burning desire to serve and be a part of the military. And those dreams had come true. I had trained. I had fought. I had led an incredible group of men through a tough deployment. What was next? My superiors made me a very attractive offer, asking me to stay in the Army and take the next step of advancement. But I knew that an unmistakable shift had taken place. The fire was gone. To anyone on the outside, I appeared to be coping well with the emotional taxation and trauma brought about by the events of the past few months. But internally, I could not will myself to feel anything. No passion or drive to continue down this path, no excitement, no sadness, no happiness, no regret. I felt utter and complete nothingness.

The dreams that had inspired me as I sat in my college classroom taking the LSATs, the ambition that pushed me to swim and run those cold, hard miles in the Florida gulf, the passion that compelled me to give up a promising career in order to enlist, all that was gone. The only prick of sensitivity I felt inside was my love for Cole. He was still just a baby, all the makings of a strong man wrapped in a tiny package. My boy probably wouldn't even recognize me when I returned home, but I promised myself that would change. My son could not, and would not, grow up without a father. I wanted to be a part of his life, to watch him get older, to teach him what it takes to be a man in this world. That led me to the decision that this deployment would be my last, and I began to make plans to retire from the military for good. I was proud of all that I had accomplished and satisfied with my contribution to the mission at hand. I loved my men and knew that Legion was comprised of an incredible and unique group of individuals. It was an honor to have had the opportunity to lead them. But it was time for that chapter of my life to end.

In early January, I boarded the plane that would take me home for good. Sitting in my seat, I was only aware of the total void I felt inside. Some part of me had died in that place. I was still the same man on the outside—smiling, laughing, and taking charge. But inside there was a blank, vacant space devoid of feeling. The earth beneath me disappeared as the plane ascended, and I wondered if a piece of Jeff Morris would be forever left behind.

Upon landing, I hopped on a bus that would take me to the field where the 'welcome home' ceremony would be held. It was freezing cold that day as I walked onto the field, my eyes searching for the sight of my son. A small group of familiar faces appeared, smiling and ready to greet me. I hugged each person, glad to see them all. Meeting each of their eyes, I could see how grateful they were to have me home, but they were obviously at a loss for what to say to me after all I had been through. But then I turned to Cole. I leaned in close to my son who was no longer a baby, but a stout toddler. I had convinced Crissy not to cut his hair until I got home, and as a result, Cole had grown a magnificent mullet. That long patch of hair running down his tiny neck brought a smile to my face.

Crissy held him out toward me and I reached for him, but he quickly turned away and buried his shaggy head into her shoulder. He didn't know me. After all, his father had been gone for fifteen months. I reached for him again, and he turned away. But on the third attempt, he came to me. I felt his little body in my arms and inhaled his nearness. And somewhere in that vast sea of numbness inside, a flicker of feeling shot through me. This. This boy. This son of mine was all I needed. Inwardly, I vowed to start a new chapter of my life, to shut out all the horrors I had witnessed and the

trauma I had been through. I vowed to leave all th.
and experiences of the past months behind me. Thaꞁ
would not touch me. I wouldn't—I couldn't—let it affect ᵢ
again.

Chapter 11

"It's impossible for words to describe what is necessary to those who do not know what horror means. Horror... Horror has a face... and you must make a friend of horror. Horror and moral terror are your friends. If they are not, then they are enemies to be feared."—Apocalypse Now

Colorado, January 2010

There was no avoiding it. I didn't want to look, but my face tilted rebelliously upward. And there they were, my pale blue eyes staring back at me in the mirror. A sound echoed in the recesses of my consciousness, the sound of agony. Of desperation. Of inhuman suffering.

As had happened so many times, in an instant I wasn't in my bathroom anymore. I was standing in the corner of a different small room, watching a man draw near to his reflection. He studied a cut on his face, running from his nose up to his cheek. I knew what he had seen that day, and what had caused that cut. I knew the terrible truth that this man was about to realize. I knew, because that man was me.

Like every time this gripped me, I shook myself back into the present moment, trying to shake the image and silence the screams. But one thing always called forth the other— my reflection and the horror I had seen.

It had been two years since I had returned from Iraq. After arriving home in January of 2008, I immersed myself in the task of building a new life. I wasted no time driving to Fort Hood and signing the papers that solidified my decision to leave the Army. As soon as I drove out of the gate, I pulled onto the side of the road and changed my watch from military to civilian time.

By April 25th of that year, I had accepted a job with a medical device company and moved to Sunnyvale, California. The job required several months of training, followed by many more months of travel. Because of this, Crissy and I didn't see the need to uproot her and Cole just yet. I made the move alone. She planned to join me for the summer months, when her work as a school teacher would be done. It was hard to leave Crissy again so quickly, but in some ways we were more accustomed to being apart than together. The majority of our relationship had been long distance and we quickly fell back into that comfortable cadence. I was fortunate to have one of the men from my second deployment, Lenny Denaro, join me in taking a job with this company. Lenny was good looking, charismatic, and funny as hell, making him a perfect candidate for the position. It was nice to have a familiar face nearby.

The job proved to be both the best and worst situation for me. The travel allowed me ample time to be alone and to think, something that felt welcome after the year I had just been through. But it also allowed me to remain in that transient mindset I had operated within for so long—living out of a suitcase, not putting down roots, refusing to get too attached to anything. It also allowed Crissy and me to delay the inevitable—coming to terms with the state of our relationship. We promised that once I was done with training and traveling, we'd settle down and give our best efforts to repairing our marriage.

I completed the necessary training for the job, spent several months on the road, and then accepted a full-time position that had opened up in Colorado under a man named Jim Butler. I liked Jim immediately. In July of 2009, I moved to Windsor, Colorado, a town at roughly five thousand feet of elevation in the northern part of the state, near Fort Collins. Crissy put our house in Austin on the market and planned to join me, along with Cole, as soon as possible. Colorado would be our new start, we said. On the surface, we liked the idea of trying to make things work between us. We had been waiting so many years for the time when we'd see each other every day, when we'd devote the best of ourselves to mending our broken relationship, when we'd actually start building a life together. We knew it wasn't going to work, but we had to try.

Crissy and Cole moved in with me Labor Day night. Cole was now three and I cherished the ability to finally see him more often. Although he had his toddler moments, he was a fun, happy-go-lucky kid, and it was a blast to spend so much time with him. In late October, we had an early snowfall, a good twenty inches, and we bought Cole a huge, puffy, onesie-style thermal jacket and took him out into that wonderland of white. Soon he was making snow angels, his cheeks pink from the cold, and building his first snowman. I'll always remember that day.

But though Crissy and I had promised ourselves and each other that we would try, we didn't. Not really. Our efforts to reconnect were lackluster at best. The cavern of emotional distance that we had slowly created between us throughout the years seemed too daunting to close. A few months later, Crissy flew with Cole to Austin to help with her new nephew, and I drove down to spend the holiday weekend with them and with her parents. Things in our relationship had been coming to a head, and we knew that we needed to talk. We stole away from the happy huddle of relatives that had gathered at her parents' home, picked up a coffee at the nearest coffee shop, and then parked on the street in front of the house to have the conversation that we'd both been avoiding.

The neighborhood was a nice area in the suburbs, with a park and a greenbelt across the street. It was late evening by this point, and we sat there under the streetlights in our SUV, taking advantage of the time away from the others. We had argued and fought many times before, but this was different. We actually talked that night. Yet during the conversation, I felt a change take place inside of me. I knew instinctively that we had crossed the point from which there would be no return. After a little while, I hopped out of the car and silently went upstairs. Everyone else was already asleep. I packed my suitcase and walked quietly into the room where Cole was sleeping. Something about the way he was lying there so peacefully pierced my heart. I didn't want him to ever feel the effects of his parents' damaged relationship. There had to be a way to protect him from feeling the pain I had felt as a child while witnessing the unrest and brokenness between my parents. Leaning down to kiss his little head, I whispered, *"Son, things will never be the same again. But always know that Daddy loves you and I will always be there for you."*

I tiptoed downstairs and was startled to see Crissy's mom awake. She began asking questions, wondering why I was leaving. Crissy's stepfather joined us and offered to drive me to the airport. Then Crissy saw me with my suitcase in hand. She began to beg and plead with me to stay. Emotions ran high and started to escalate further. All I could think about was needing a quiet place, needing peace. In the darkness, the edge of a wooded area was visible, bordering the neighborhood, and I left the house with suitcase in hand and started walking toward it. Away from the chaos, away from the pain, disappearing into the protection that the trees provided. There was no trail, and no easy path through the brush, but I walked for over a mile until I emerged near a local pizza shop. A man was inside, closing up. He came outside as I approached, looking concerned, asked, "Are you okay, buddy?"

I looked down at my arms, covered in scrapes and scratches from my trek through the woods, and the suitcase in my hand. "I'm alright, man. It's just been... a rough night. I need to call a cab."

He didn't ask questions, he just offered me a beer and a place to sit inside while I waited for a cab to take me to the airport. I was thankful. A small act of kindness can mean everything when your world is crumbling. I gratefully drank the beer and welcomed his company as he sat beside me, talking about football, distracting me from all of the things I could have been thinking at that moment. The taxi arrived and carried me off. It was midnight by the time I arrived at the airport, and everything inside was closed, looking dark and empty. I took a seat and then waited for my morning flight. Sleep never came; I just sat there in that quiet, nearly deserted terminal. All the feeling, all the anger, all the disappointment, all the sadness, it was all gone. I was blank inside. And so I sat in silence.

As I found myself staring down a divorce, I became determined to find a way to get back to Texas in order to be closer to Cole. I wasn't going to let him grow up without me in his life. When morning came, I called my boss, Jim Butler, and told him that I needed to figure out some way to move as soon as a position opened in Texas. He was more than gracious and told me that he would do everything he could to get me closer to my son while keeping my job.

When I returned home to Colorado after that trip, something changed. An unshakeable darkness fell over me. I didn't drink myself to sleep, or take drugs, or sleep with strangers.

My darkness crept up silently but surely, choking out all feeling. I woke up, went to work, worked out, and then headed straight home and went to sleep. Day after day. I could think of nothing beyond what was right in front of me. All drive and passion for life had been removed. I only existed to accomplish the tasks that each day provided. To those on the outside looking in, I didn't exhibit signs of depression or dysfunction. I worked hard at my job and put on a friendly face throughout my days. But internally, I was sinking further and further into a hole, a hole that went much deeper than despair over a failed marriage. That hole contained everything I had pent up and stuffed down and willed to go away, and it pulled me deeper and deeper into itself, further and further away from the man I used to be. It didn't assault me with pain, it simply lured me into an inner nothingness, like floating in silent, sunless space. I no longer even felt numb, only empty.

When your internal world is nothing but a black void, brief moments of feeling stick out vividly. I remember my boss, Jim, inviting me to join him for dinner or calling just to talk with me on the phone—a small ray of light invading my world. In the same way, I remember Wednesday lunches at a local Mexican restaurant with a friend, Misty Lever, that gave me something to look forward to. Misty and her husband David's kindness towards me was a gleam in the darkness. I remember another friend, Marcus, calling me on a Saturday morning and telling me to meet him at the airport the next morning. He told me that he had two Denver Broncos tickets with incredible seats, he was flying in from Austin for the game, and he wanted to share the experience with me. I met him at the airport and we drove to Denver, tailgated with a few perfect strangers, watched the game, and then returned back to the airport for his flight home. That night was a glimmer of hope, a hint of how things should be different.

But after these flickers of light would shine into my world, I would return to the darkness again. I didn't know how to crawl out of the hole after traveling so deeply into it. In many ways, I felt like it could have been worse. Experiencing total emptiness seemed preferable to the things that many of my men were battling upon their return. In comparison to the manifestation of their struggles, wasn't I doing alright? I often snapped back into leadership mode throughout that time, making calls to the families of those who had died on the anniversaries and talking on the phone with men who called me in turmoil over the events we had all lived through together. I could hear the pain and torment in those voices. Sometimes they asked hard questions in moments of drunken honesty. Sometimes the voices told me of the gun in their hand and their dying will to live. I was strong for my men, continuing to uphold the responsibility I felt to care for them. *You're fine, Jeff,* I told myself. *Things could be much worse. You're handling life well, from the tough deployment you went through, to the divorce. You work hard at your job and you don't drink yourself to sleep, so doesn't that mean you're stable enough to be a rock for the others to lean on?*

But as the winter of 2009 descended, vivid memories and images began to invade my vacant inner world. At first I tried to push them away. But they kept coming. The mundane rhythm of my days left no distractions for me to cling to as a means of avoidance. The sight of any tall, young man brought the sickening sound of Coon's screams into my head. Memories of the men floated into my mind. I replayed each detail of March 15th, each choice I had made, each order I had given. Feelings of guilt arose. *I should have been with my men that day. I shouldn't have stayed back. Surely I could have done something to keep my men safe.* I thought of PFC Arnold's quick obedience at the sound of my order for him to take my place. My place. My seat. It should have been me. What would his family think if they knew I should have been the one, not him, to die?

Mirrors taunted me daily. Every time I met my eyes in the reflection, all I could hear was that haunting sound of Coon's last moments before he died. And then all I could see was that man standing in front of a mirror, looking at a gash on his face, realizing the cause of that torn skin, experiencing the true meaning of horror. I understood that man was me, but when my mind flashed back, it was not as if I was reliving those moments, but rather observing them off to the side in that small room.

And so I began to shave my head. It seemed like a simple solution. If I could avoid the mirror, I could avoid the pain it evoked. For a little while, it seemed to work. But then in moments of internal contradiction, when that sense of total void and emptiness would overtake me, I would look into that mirror willfully, daring the pain to surface. Sometimes feeling pain is the only way to know if you are capable of feeling anything at all. This was pain I could induce at will, giving me the sense of control.

However, other emotions spilled out without warning, leaving me feeling powerless. Once, while sitting in the Denver airport, waiting for my flight, a man with bagpipes began to pass slowly down the walkway, playing a beautiful melody. I don't know what he was doing or why he was there, but I know that tears poured down my cheeks and memories of the memorials for the men that Legion had lost filled my mind.

But moments of pain or sadness were only momentary, the black emptiness swiftly swallowing me up as soon as the feelings dissipated. Other than connecting with Cole, I refused to engage in emotional intimacy with any human being. For the most part, that way was more comfortable. As the months passed, signs appeared that I wasn't alright, that

I wasn't the person that I used to be. But I wasn't ready to let anyone see the dark hole that was my home. So I made every effort to keep other people at arm's length. On occasion, when I felt lonely, I would send a Facebook message or text to an old friend. This form of communication allowed me to hide behind a keyboard and screen. I could control when I turned it on and when I shut it off.

Not long after Christmas, I received a message from an old friend from my college days, a woman named Shay. *"Hey stranger, how are you doing?"* the message read. I smiled and simply sent back, *"Hey stranger, how are YOU doing?"* We messaged back and forth for a while, catching up on all the years that had gone by. We exchanged phone numbers and talked the following night. Shay and I quickly discovered that we shared a common bond, the fact that certain aspects of our lives uncannily echoed one another. We shared similar experiences, particularly pertaining to relationships, and we both found comfort in talking with another person who could relate so fully. In the following months we talked on the phone often, sometimes for a few minutes, sometimes for an hour or more. In that time, as the darkness within me grew and threatened to overtake me, my conversations with Shay pushed away the shadows for a few moments of my day. A phone call doesn't seem like much in the grand scheme of things, but for me, it was a lifeline that kept me from drowning.

As more time passed, I was forced to acknowledge that something was off. I felt like a shell of the man I used to be. And I felt increasingly like a hypocrite each time I put on a smile and a brave-sounding voice, giving advice and guidance to various members of Legion who called on me for help. I knew all the right things to say, but the reality was that I wasn't following my own advice. I made it sound so simple, so straightforward when I spoke to others. But internally I felt paralyzed, unable to move, unable to choose anything beyond my current state. Still, I tried.

I scheduled a session with a counselor, but was quickly repelled by his manner and methods. Willing to try spiritual sources, I even went to a local church, looking for some word, some key to unlock the door that kept me confined. I would wait in the lobby, sipping a cup of coffee and reading a newspaper until the singing and announcement portion of the service was over, and then I would slip into the back of the congregation to hear the sermon. Week after week, nothing resonated with me. Then one Sunday, the pastor introduced a brand new series that he was beginning about inner walls that people erect around themselves.

"It takes a long time to build up these walls, doesn't it?" he said from the pulpit. "Maybe you've built walls to protect yourself, and maybe it seems like they will always be there. But you can be encouraged. Those walls can quickly come crumbling down with the right tools in hand."

The pastor's words deeply stirred something in me. But I never returned. The remainder of his series promised to uncover the key to knocking those walls down. And I wasn't ready for that.

The months that Crissy and I had spent apart only solidified my decision to end things for good. In the spring of 2010, I downsized from the house we had been living in to a small, one-bedroom apartment. I packed up all of our belongings in a U-Haul, and drove down to Austin to give it all back to her. I kept a spare mattress, a couch, and one of the televisions. That was it. *Don't put down roots. Don't attach yourself to anything you can't pick up and move at a moment's notice.* This became my mantra. It seemed to me that all the bad things that had happened in my life occurred when I let other people in too close. So I created my own little world of total self-reliance. I repeated the same tasks each day—work, workout, sleep. I declined most invitations for social gatherings. I didn't furnish my little apartment, finding myself more comfortable with the notion that I could pack my things and move anywhere at any time. The impermanence of my arrangement fed my transient mindset. I answered to no one but myself.

That August, I finally received the call that I had been waiting for. Amy Sullivan was a manager in north Texas with my company and she was calling with good news. "Jeff, there's a position that's opened up in Tyler, Texas, that we think you'd be great for." She told me about the position, but honestly I was already sold by the "Texas" part. "What do you think? Are you interested?"

I had never been to Tyler before, but the knowledge that it was closer to Cole was all I needed. "Yes, I'll take it." After thanking my boss, Jim, for helping me land the position, I packed my things and moved.

That change provided a sharp dichotomy in my life. On the one hand, I could see Cole more often. He was the one and only beam of light and love that consistently shone into my dark world since returning home from Iraq. On the other hand, I was now living in a town where I knew no one. Though I worked to isolate myself in Colorado, I still had acquaintances that I had grown familiar with as well as Jim's companionship. Jim always seemed to have a knack for knowing just the right time to invite me to dinner or to join him in an activity that he had planned. He had a way of breaking through my resistance towards friendship, leaving me no time to pull away or decline his invitations. In Tyler, I didn't have that. And I felt myself retreating even further into my black hole.

Texas is known for its hot weather, full of sunshine. But during those first months in Tyler, all I remember were cold, bleak days. I gravitated toward the gloomy, overcast weather, as if the universe was imitating the shadows inside me. I executed the necessary duties that each day presented, using my friendly smile and lighthearted tone as an effective decoy. I made the four-hour drive to Austin almost every weekend to see Cole, grateful to be in proximity to him.

As the months passed, I recognized how isolated I had become from regular interaction with other adults. Even in my current mindset, I was self-aware enough to know that I couldn't live a life of solitary confinement, and I refused to allow myself to become dysfunctional or removed from society. And so I carefully arranged my schedule to create short social encounters, administering small doses of interaction with other people as if tending to a basic human need such as water, sleep, or food. I went to certain restaurants on certain nights, to ensure that there wouldn't be crowds. A sense of control accompanied my self-created routine. I mastered the art of being able to walk in, have a drink, order my food, crack a few jokes with the bartender, eat, pay my check, and walk out within fifteen minutes. For those brief moments, it was like I was a different person, or perhaps just a distant expression of the man I once was, a man I couldn't allow myself to be anymore. I told jokes, I laughed, I talked about life. And it felt good. But if conversations extended past my comfort zone, in length or subject matter, I quickly left, citing excuses such as needing to call my son or go somewhere else.

As soon as I got back in the car, I would turn on the song "Hand Covers Bruise" by Trent Reznor and Atticus Ross and then "Crazy Horse" by Black Label Society and let them play, the haunting and then pounding music immediately returning me to my world of darkness. Those familiar melodies brought tears to my eyes, bringing back memories and all the pain, grief, and loss I held inside. I felt the need, it seemed, to remind myself that a carefree life was simply not in the cards for me, it was not my reality. That engaging man who talked and laughed used to be me—moments of sadness and emptiness the exception. But now the black hole had become my norm, and moments of light or joy the exception. I felt that there was no reason to waste time remaining in that happy world of human connection when I knew that I wasn't meant to stay there. And so I played those songs and let them pull me back into the shadows, ensuring that by the time I pulled into my garage I was planted squarely back in what I felt was the real world.

Music held great power over me, evoking emotions that otherwise remained locked away. Upon hearing a melody such as the songs I listened to while driving or the bagpipes I heard in the airport, tears would stream down my face. But in other situations, when tears seemed appropriate, such as the funeral of my beloved grandfather, not a drop would fall from my eyes. Despite the deep love and connection I felt for him, even surrounded by the mournful sobs of my family as they grieved his death, I felt incapable of shedding a tear.

I watched the film *Apocalypse Now* many times during those months, obsessed with one particular scene, one particular stream of dialogue:

"I've seen horrors... horrors that you've seen. But you have no right to call me a murderer. You have a right to kill me. You have a right to do that... but you have no right to judge me. It's impossible for words to describe what is necessary to those who do not know what horror means. Horror... Horror has a face... and you must make a friend of horror. Horror and moral terror are your friends. If they are not, then they are enemies to be feared. They are truly enemies. I remember when I was with Special Forces... seems a thousand centuries ago. We went into a camp to inoculate some children. We left the camp after we had inoculated the children for polio, and this old man came running after us and he was crying. He couldn't see. We went back there, and they had come and hacked off every inoculated arm. There they were in a pile. A pile of little arms. And I remember... I... I... I cried, I wept like some grandmother. I wanted to tear my teeth out; I didn't know what I wanted to do. And I want to remember it. I never want to forget it... I never want to forget. And then I realized... like I was shot... like I was shot with a diamond... a diamond bullet right through my forehead. And I thought, my God... the genius of that! The genius! The will to do that! Perfect, genuine, complete, crystalline, pure. And then I realized they were stronger than we, because they could stand that these were not monsters, these were men... trained cadres. These men who fought with their hearts, who had families, who had children, who were filled with love... but they had the strength... the strength... to do that. If I had ten divisions of those men, our troubles here would be over very quickly. You have to have men who are moral... and at the same time who are able to utilize their primordial instincts to kill without feeling... without passion... without judgment... without judgment! Because it's judgment that defeats us."

I wanted to know how to make peace, to make friends with the horror I had witnessed. I didn't desire a seared conscience or to make friends with cruelty, I simply wanted to know how to accept the things I had seen, the things I had been through. I searched for resolution to questions that simply could not be answered. *Why am I still breathing when other good men are not? Why do I have the privilege of watching my son grow up when so many other loving fathers will never have that chance? How do I reconcile the fact that a man died because I ordered him to switch seats with me?* I told myself that it wasn't my fault, I told myself I shouldn't carry that guilt. I asked myself why, out of 999 decisions I made that turned out alright, I chose to focus on the one that ended badly. So I fought for answers. I fought for understanding. I wasn't ready to accept the things that had happened.

One night while sitting at one of my regular restaurants, I heard a rather boisterous voice from the other end of the bar. It came from a tall blonde—exuberant and friendly. The bartender introduced me to her. Her name was Charity. We fell into friendly conversation, and within five minutes she was convinced that I was destined to be best friends with her husband.

"You need to meet him, just trust me on this," she said with a grin. "You'll get along great. What are you doing tomorrow night?"

Unprepared for this question, I admitted, "I guess I don't have any particular plans."

"Perfect. Come back here the same time tomorrow, and I'll be back here with John so you two can meet." The expression on her face made it clear she would not take no for an answer, and I agreed and left the restaurant wondering what had just happened. It was far outside my comfort zone, agreeing to participate in something of a blind date to explore the possibility of becoming good friends with another fellow, but Charity's take-charge, gregarious manner somehow forced me to say yes. When I returned the following night I did hit it off with her husband, just as she had promised, making them my first friends in Tyler.

While out to dinner one evening, they convinced me that I had to try CrossFit—an exercise class that was gaining momentum all over the country and was growing popular in Tyler. I tried one class and liked it immediately. At the core of CrossFit's philosophy is the idea of becoming physically equipped in all aspects of fitness, combining a variety of movements, including gymnastics, olympic lifting, high-intensity cardio, strength-building work, and much more. It is designed to increase strength, speed, endurance, coordination, skill, balance, and stamina. Each day a new workout is released, what CrossFitters refer to as the "WOD" (Workout Of the Day), and each class, led by a specially certified trainer, completes it. The workouts were no joke and I loved the challenge. The classes weren't held in a shiny, climate-controlled gym, but rather in a small building equipped with barbells, a tall rig for doing pull-ups and other gymnastic movements, ropes, kettlebells, and a few other essential items.

Perhaps it is the close quarters, the raw conditions, or the fact that we all endure the same fierce workout side by side, but CrossFit has a way of creating a tight-knit community. After a few months, I made friends with a handful of people and often received invitations to dinners, barbecues, and outings. And I found myself saying yes. It was nice to be with people. But I couldn't get away from the fact that I felt distant and removed, unable to shake the shadows that loomed within me. On the outside, I was happy, friendly, and engaging. When people saw my tattoos and heard that I was in the military, they were quickly intrigued. I was the guy that had cool stories to tell, and people seemed to like having me around. But I maintained my vigilance, carefully ensuring that no one got too close, that no one asked questions that I didn't want to answer. I prided myself in being honest, in refusing to tell a lie, so I navigated conversations in such a way that I would never be confronted with a question that I wasn't prepared to answer. The most effective way to do that seemed to be implementing a preemptive strategy. I would be the first to offer a story, show pictures, or pull up something relevant to my deployment from the internet. In doing so, I could maintain control of the conversation. If I threw out a few exciting stories with an edge of violence, it would satisfy most people's curiosity and hold further questioning at bay. And so I offered the pictures and videos as a shield and as something of an explanation for who I was, for the man that I had become. I quickly followed up these brief glimpses into my story with the statement, "It shapes me but it doesn't define me." But despite how much I wanted that to be true, it wasn't.

A few of the married women took it upon themselves to set me up with single girls they knew, but I pushed back in no uncertain terms. "I promise you, I will only disappoint you," I said to each woman that ventured close to my internal walls. Even the promise of romance or a night of passion could not dissuade me from my stance. I believed that this new version of me was incapable of being in a relationship of any kind. I respected each of the women who approached me far too much to lead them on, pretending that somehow I could engage in any type of emotional intimacy when I knew just how inadequate my capacity was.

Although my days were filled with more interaction, more people, more time with Cole, more money, and more activity, the feeling of complete emptiness remained. In a room full of laughing, happy people I still felt isolated and alone. The darkness had pressed down on me for so long, I began to accept that it would be there forever. *Maybe this is it. Maybe this is just who I am.* It wasn't what I wanted, it wasn't the life I had envisioned as a young man, full of hopes and dreams. Wasn't I the all-American boy who gave his best years to serve his country, who always tried to do the right thing? And here I was divorced, living alone, and unable to emerge from the shadows within.

I went home to Florida to see my parents for Christmas in 2011. One evening after dinner, I sat on their couch and my mom sat down next to me. When she looked into my eyes, tears welled up in hers until they poured down her face.

"Mom, what's wrong?" Worried, I waited as she regained her composure.

"Jeff, I've always said that your big blue eyes are the light of my life and whenever I look at them, I just know everything is going to be okay," she said. "But when I look at them now, the light is gone. My baby boy looks dead inside."

My mother paused, the tears threatening to spill again, "And for the first time, I'm not so sure that everything is going to be okay."

Chapter 12

"The journey home is never a direct route; it is, in fact, always circuitous, and somewhere along the way, we discover that the journey is more significant than the destination and that the people we meet along the way will be the traveling companions of our memories forever."—Nelson DeMille, Up Country

Tyler, TX, Winter 2012

I shifted uncomfortably on the small loveseat, my eyes wandering to scan the wall beside me, generously lined with books. Before me, behind a modest desk, sat a man who was about to know parts of my story that few did. He watched me, patiently expectant. He had red hair, an unhurried manner, and something nonthreatening in his eyes, kindness perhaps.

I knew it was my turn to talk. After all, he was the well-respected counselor, while I was the one who had requested our meeting. It had been a few months since I sat on my parents' couch in Florida, a few months since my mom told me that her baby boy's eyes looked dead inside. I hadn't committed to seeing a counselor right away; nothing massive changed that night. But her words gnawed at me in the days and weeks following that conversation. If your own mother says you have changed, isn't that the ultimate proof that you have?

I cleared my throat and then began. Not one for shrouding my words in vagueness or mystery, I saw no need to string the counselor along with a series of hints, hoping that he would draw me out with just the right question. And so in that small room, on that loveseat, I told him everything.

When I finished, there were no tears streaming down my face. I didn't feel an instant connection with the man in front of me simply from sharing my most sacred pain with him. I just sat there, almost daring him to say something that would drive me away, something that would give me license to walk out and never return. He stared back at me and didn't say anything for a few moments. Then he cleared his throat before speaking, "Jeff, even Hollywood could not imagine something that messed up. This is something that you are going to have to learn to live with."

His response caught me off-guard. No one had ever simply acknowledged the horror of the things I had seen. The memories, the images, the phantom screams, it had all swirled inside my head for so long. But here it was, laid out in the open, filling the space between my seat and his. *Even Hollywood could not imagine something that messed up.* His words weren't profound or elaborate. But somehow they brought relief. I allowed another human being a glimpse into my world and my pain, and he saw what I saw.

This is something that you are going to have to learn to live with. He didn't promise that he could fix me or talk about his qualifications. With that one simple statement, he put the responsibility to emerge from my darkness squarely on my shoulders. Right where it belonged. He could help, he could guide, but the choice to find resolution would ultimately be mine. His words were honest, not filled with plush promises void of substance. It made me feel sure-footed enough to trust him, enough to agree to take the next step. And for the first time, I felt just the smallest semblance of hope that this pain and grief wouldn't overshadow me forever.

"When you experience the flashback of that day in the bathroom, looking at the scar on your face in the mirror, are you looking directly in the mirror or are you off to the side, observing yourself looking into the mirror?" he asked.

I explained how it was the latter, how it was not as if I was standing in front of that mirror, but rather as if I was another person, standing in the corner, watching myself look into the mirror. I felt it odd that I saw things that way, and told him so.

"It actually makes perfect sense," he said. "What that tells me is that you still haven't accepted what happened. You can't deal with things until they are real and they aren't real until you accept them. Before we do anything, we need to get you to a place where you can look into the mirror again."

He was right. As long as I remained the witness in the corner, the observer of my trauma, the things I had been through would never become a reality I could accept. I began to meet with this counselor every few weeks, each session a small step forward into acceptance. He didn't call it a healing process, which would denote that I was somehow wounded or broken. He called it an awakening, a term which resonated deeply with me.

But awakening out of the darkness of a deep and empty sleep is not an easy task. As you begin to stir, you realize that the thick fog that encompassed you for so long also served as insulation from pain. As your eyes begin to open and feelings begin to revive, you finally experience the full force of the pain you avoided for so long.

As I struggled through the process of awakening, the final details of mine and Crissy's divorce came to a head. Though we had been separated for some time, we had never legally finalized our divorce. It was long overdue. And, as with most people's experience of divorce, it was complicated. Why is it that the moment you decide to stop fighting for one another, you fight against each other instead? When you rip the interwoven fabric of relationship, finances, and parenting, it all seems to unravel.

Those months were hard months. As my deadened nerves came back to life, I felt things like I hadn't before. I felt the pain and horror of many Iraq experiences in fresh ways. I felt the misery of my failed marriage and the frustration of trying to finalize it. It felt good to be awake, but sometimes I longed for the empty sleep. On one particular day, feelings from the divorce and pain from the past collided, creating an inner turmoil that wouldn't calm. Once again a patch of woods presented itself to me, and I walked in, seeking peace and solitude. For hours I walked in those woods, pausing every so often to sit and attempt to sort out the things I felt inside. I was fighting to stay awake, fighting to feel, fighting the magnetic pull of that dark hole within me that greedily tried to drag me back. I walked. And walked. I sat and thought. And then walked some more. I finally exited the woods, many hours later, to find my phone filled with a bombardment of calls and text messages, wondering where I was and whether I was okay. But how do you explain the need to walk among the trees, to silence the chaos inside?

The struggle was intense. The counselor was like a signpost pointing me in the right direction, but I still had to fight to emerge from the shadows that had held me back for so long.

And then there was light. It didn't come in all at once with blinding force. But it came. And I slowly began to notice the shadows around me disappearing. I began to accept the things that I had been through, accept the horror that I had seen, accept each part of my story without fighting it. All of it was a part of me. It was my reality. And for the first time,

I felt like I had the power to choose what I was going to do with it.

"I think I get what you're saying now," I said one day a few months later during my counseling session. "Acceptance is not a one-time choice. Every day I have to choose to accept all the things that I have been through, all the aspects of who I am."

He smiled. "You got it. But we're not done yet. You've made some pretty significant self-observations and steps forward. You're an educated guy, you speak well, and I remember early on you told me that you were unsure of what I could do to help you because I had not seen the things you had seen. I admired you for saying that. And you're right, I haven't been through what you've been through. The things you've seen would rival anyone's worst experiences. But if you can awaken, if you can move past this, you can show anyone that no matter what they've been through, they can too. And I want you to start thinking about how your story could impact others. So I have a challenge for you. I want you to share your story with someone or maybe a small group of people that you know you can trust, people that are outside of the military. And perhaps you'll find that others can relate to your story and what you've been through more than you think."

The opportunity to accept his challenge opened up just a few weeks later. A small group of close friends made plans to gather together for an evening, hosted by Mel and Fran Morgan, one of the couples I knew from Premier CrossFit. I grilled a platter of ribs and brought them with me, knowing as I walked up the steps and into the house that this was the chance that I had been looking for. I grabbed a beer as soon as possible, hoping to calm my anxiety about pulling down the walls that had protected me for so long. One beer didn't quite do the trick, so I had another. And maybe another. Finally, after eating the evening's spread of food, everyone gathered casually in the living room and I saw my opening—it was now or never. I cleared my throat.

When you tell people a few cool stories from your military experience, they like it and they admire and respect you. But I feared that if I shared honestly, if I pulled back the layers and let them see a true glimpse into the horrors I had experienced, they would push me away, repelled by my story. However, this was part of the process, part of my awakening, and I had come too far to stop now.

I shared with them the fact that I had been getting counseling and told them about the counselor's challenge to me. And then I just started talking, pouring out everything I had held in for so long. I talked and they listened, getting up every so often to refresh their drinks. I didn't stop until my story had been laid bare: the good, the tragic, the heroic, the ugly, the horrible. When I finished, no one said a word. We all sat in silence, the weight of honesty between us.

Then Kyle Ischy, one of the men that I often worked out with, rose from his chair and walked over to me. Kyle was known for his aggressively heavy lifting and the ability to hold his liquor better than most people. He walked to where I was seated and I stood, feeling exposed and vulnerable. He faced me and said, "I don't know what to say right now. I don't think anybody knows what to say. But in my family, when we're faced with times like this, when no one knows what to say, we all stop and pray." He took hold of me and then said a prayer, everyone in the room bowing his or her head along with him. Then he wrapped me into a hug and said, "I know that was hard to share. Thank you for trusting us with this. I love you and we all love you."

I looked around to see the faces of people that I could now truly call friends. I saw Mel and Fran, Chad and Hayle Hudson, Kyle, John and Charity, and a few others. They had listened to my story, and even when I showed them the entirety of who I was, they didn't run away; instead, they drew in even closer.

"I have an idea," said a voice from the corner of the room. It was my good friend John Wilmoth. "Why don't we get together and do a workout in honor of your boys? We could call it Legion 8." Everyone jumped on the idea, especially me. After feeling so much numbness and emptiness inside, the thought of having the chance to channel this story into action, into something that I could get my heart, mind, and body involved in, sounded perfect.

So together, in the late hours of the night, we put our somewhat drunken minds together and created a CrossFit workout to honor the men. Sometimes when you go through something hard, you just need to remember to hang on, to not let go. I suggested that we utilize CrossFit movements that would be particularly taxing on the grip to demonstrate the struggle of holding on through tough times. I wanted that struggle manifested in my body, I wanted to feel it in my hands—the struggle felt for so many years by the families of those who had died. I wanted a workout that would push me to the brink of giving up, as life had so many times. I wanted it to embody the fight that I, and countless others, had faced, the fight to hold on when all strength is gone.

We worked through the late hours of the night to create a fitting workout. We planned to have eight rounds of eight different movements that would be done in sets of eight repetitions at a time. The workout would include lifts and strength movements, basic gymnastics, as well as a bit of high cardio. I wanted the workout to be long, with numerous repetitions, creating something of a tiny microcosm of life, something that captured the pain and struggle it is to fight through the aftermath of tragedy. One more rep, one more day without a father, fiancé, brother, husband, or son. Holding onto the bar when you're exhausted, holding onto hope when you feel like giving up. Digging deep and pressing through the pain when you just want it all to go away. Making the choice to do one rep and then another and then another, making the choice to move forward day after day after day. This was the fight I wanted exemplified throughout the workout. We finally finished piecing together what we believed would be a great workout and planned to meet and do it side-by-side in the near future.

When I woke up the next day, I looked at our plans again, assessing the fruits of our efforts. In the sober light of the morning, I realized that we had concocted a brutal workout. I brought it to one of the Premier CrossFit trainers, Chris Hughes, and asked his opinion on it, also sharing the idea behind it. He was all for it, but he suggested a few minor tweaks that would help with the flow of the workout and make it more grip-intensive. Then he offered to try it that week to test it before we did it as a group. He texted me a few days later to let me know that he was about to start it. Not twenty minutes after I read his text, he called me. "Are you already done?" I asked, surprised.

"No, man, we've got to reduce the suggested weight for the barbell work, I just did four rounds and I'm smoked," he said. "There's no way most people could get through eight rounds of this." So we made a few more changes.

Finally, the Legion 8 WOD was officially created. It consisted of:

8 Rounds For Time Of:

8 Thrusters (75/55 lbs)

8 Chest-to-Bar Pull-Ups

8 Clapping Push-Ups

8 Power Snatches (75/55 lbs)

8 Knees-to-Elbows

8 Sumo Deadlift High-Pulls (75/55 lbs)

8 Handstand Push-Ups

8 Toes-to-Bar

Then 800 meter Run

When the owners of Premier CrossFit, Cune and Michelle Peña, caught wind of what we were doing, they jumped in without hesitation, helping us schedule a time to do it together on a Saturday a few weeks from then. When Cune is excited about something, it's contagious. With him on board, the number of people who planned to participate grew quickly. Michelle took charge of handling all of the logistics involved in actually pulling off the big idea. I contacted a few of the men from my unit as well as a few of the families of those who had died, informed them of what we were doing, and invited them to join us if they desired. Someone asked if I planned to share something before the workout, something that explained why we were there and what we were doing. I felt anxious at the thought of standing in front of a group of people and exposing a part of me that had been hidden for so long. After all, I was new to living in the light. But I agreed and began to prepare what I planned to say.

I wanted to honor the men, but somehow words seemed so inadequate. Then the idea came to me of making a slideshow, with images from the deployment and pictures of each of the eight men who died. I went to work creating a slideshow in the days leading up to the Legion 8 workout. I chose background music, a sad but hauntingly beautiful melody played by bagpipes that was performed at the men's memorial. I dug through old pictures, reliving not just the sadness for the ones we lost but also the laughter we shared, the pride we felt in serving our country, and the deep bond that connected us. For so long I had tried to forget that chapter of my life, and did everything I could to avoid it. It felt good to remember that part of me. I felt a fresh wave of grief and sorrow as I pieced together the slideshow, but it was accompanied by gratitude for the incredible men that I had the opportunity to know and serve with.

The day of the Legion 8 WOD finally came. I expected to see my small group of friends from CrossFit and maybe a few others. But the closer we got to the starting time, the more people kept walking through the doors, ready to participate. Lynda Kagan, SGT Ryan Green's mother, and Danny Roland, Lynda's nephew and SGT Ryan Green's cousin, traveled into Tyler to be a part of the event as well as several of the men from Legion, including Orlando Garcia, Mike Krayer, James Mills, and Eduardo Jiminez.

Once everyone had gathered, finding seats on the ground amongst the ropes, weights, and rig, I stood. I dimmed the lights and then played the slideshow I had created, projected onto the dark, rough gym walls. I stood back as it played, not sure what to feel as a roomful of people sat watching pictures slide by of the smiling faces of each of the eight men. When it was over, someone raised the lights and I gazed out across the group sitting in front of me. Tear-stained faces looked back.

I walked to the middle of the room and opened my mouth, uncertain where to start. Somehow, I managed to stutter and stumble through the history of Legion and the story of the men who died. In that context, I thought it best not to go into certain details of my own personal story like I had when it was a smaller group of trusted friends. But even still, raw emotions surfaced quickly as I spoke, my voice breaking. I held back my tears, up until I began to introduce 1SG Orlando Garcia. As I looked over at him, memories flooded through me of standing beside him in the makeshift morgue that night over the dead bodies of our dear friends. I tried to introduce him, but the words just wouldn't come out, only tears. I couldn't speak. Orlando didn't leave me standing there alone, choking down sobs. He walked up and embraced me, his own tears flowing down his face. He had been by my side through it all. And here he was again, right next to me when I needed him. As we embraced, the entire room felt thick with emotion and the power of connection.

Then Lynda Kagan, SGT Ryan Green's mom, stood and spoke, her speech far more eloquent than mine. She ended with, "So often when we get together, we have tears in our eyes. But today we can put a smile on our face, we can sweat, we can laugh together, and we can honor our boys together."

When she finished speaking, we all stood. It was time. We quickly pulled out the necessary equipment and set the clock. And then someone called out, "Three... two... one... GO!" Suddenly the room was ablaze with electric energy, created by the sound of banging barbells and the overwhelming feeling of human love and interconnectedness. As sweat poured down my face, I thought of all the challenges that had gone before me. As I struggled to keep from letting go of the barbell, I thought of all the days that I and so many others had fought to hold on. All of the memories, all of the emotions that I had pent up now pulsed through my body as I executed each movement. This is what it feels like to be awake. This is what it feels like to be alive. My fire had returned.

And as I looked around, I realized that I was not alone. People of every age and background surrounded me, people who had been in the military and people who hadn't, people who were willing to cry with me and sweat with me. Sharing my story hadn't resulted in others pushing me away and leaving me alone. On the contrary, it was the catalyst that made my walls come crumbling down, allowing other people to see me, to touch me, to stand beside me.

We finished the workout with high fives and unforced smiles, glistening from the heart-pounding exertion and searing Texas heat. I laughed, truly laughed that day. And it felt good. For so long, I worked to push down and hide parts of my story, trying to avoid the pain of acceptance. But when I finally stopped being afraid and fully accepted everything I had been through, it felt like an oppressive weight had been lifted from my chest.

As we all stood around, catching our breath and throwing back a few cold beers, a man approached me and asked if he could talk with me for a moment. He proceeded to tell me how much it had impacted him to hear my story, to listen to me share about how I had let particular experiences from my life control and consume me. He went on to share with me his own very personal story of trauma. "Just like you, I've always said that my experience shapes me but doesn't define me," he said. "But I realized today that it is defining me. And it's time to make some meaningful changes."

I didn't realize that right there at Premier CrossFit, on a hot Saturday in Tyler, Texas, an event that would be repeated and carry on for years to come had been born. And I didn't realize that continuing to share my story through the platform that Legion 8 events created would open the door to countless other conversations like the one that had just happened. All I knew that day was that I was finally emerging from the shadows that had oppressed me for so long. I had forgotten how good it felt to be a leader and to do something that benefited others. And I basked in the light that poured into me that day.

My awakening didn't happen overnight. It didn't happen in one counseling session or one workout. But through a series of many small choices, 2011 marked the beginning of a fresh start. A hundred times I had asked myself, *How do I make peace with the horror I have seen?* And finally I had my answer. I had to face my pain, my trauma, and my scars head on and acknowledge that they will forever be part of me. I had to stand up and take ownership of every detail of my story, which meant to stop fighting and avoiding the darkness. I had to step into that looming shadow in order to step through it.

When I finally faced my reflection, when I listened to the sound of my own voice saying aloud all of the things that had happened in my life, my experiences became real to me. I was no longer the observer of my own life and memories. I could look at my reflection without flinching, owning every part of my story. I was holding the reins of my life again.

I remembered a poem that a man by the name of Frank Feely sent me during my second deployment. It read:

It's All in A State of Mind

If you think you are beaten, you are
If you think you dare not, you won't,
If you like to win, but don't think you can
It's almost a cinch you won't

If you think you'll lose, you're lost
For out in the world you'll find,
Success begins with a fellow's will
It's all in a state of mind

For many a game is lost
Ere even a play is run,
And many a coward fails
Ere even his work is begun

Think big and your deeds will grow
Think small and you'll fall behind
Think that you can and you will
It's all a state of mind

If you think you are outclassed, you are
You've got to think high to rise
You've got to be sure of yourself before
You can ever win a prize

Life battles don't always go
To the stronger or faster man
But sooner or later, the man who wins
Is the fellow who thinks he can

I read those words over and over again, allowing them to resonate deeply within me. I finally understood that though I had no control over the things that I had been through, I could control my state of mind. I could choose my outlook, my perspective, and the state of my internal world.

One of the doctors that I worked with would always walk into the operating room and say, "Alright, who's going to be a catalyst today and who's going to be a limiting factor?" That phrase stuck with me. For so long, I had allowed one point in my life to be my limiting factor, to hold me back from moving forward. But as I learned to daily choose my state of mind, my limiting factor actually became a catalyst for helping others.

Word about Legion 8 and the impact it made on those who participated spread quickly. I was featured in a prominent local magazine and was interviewed on Tyler's television station. In the weeks following the event, people approached me constantly about how much they had been inspired and touched by my story and the story behind Legion 8. I was presented with countless opportunities to hear the stories of others who felt brave enough to open up for the first time after listening to something I said. When I realized just how much of a widespread effect this was having, I felt it my obligation to devote myself to using my story, and the story of Legion 8, as a catalyst to create meaningful change in the lives of others. I didn't ask to be given a platform; it was handed to me when I least expected it. But I had wasted four years of my life feeling empty, stuck, and internally immobilized. If I could spare even one person from wasting another moment of his or her life, my endeavors would be well worth it. And so I made the choice to dedicate my life to helping others learn to look in the mirror again.

Over the course of the next several years, I led countless Legion 8 events at gyms all over the nation. Various men from my unit often accompanied me, and Lynda Kagan, SGT Ryan Green's mom, became an integral part of the movement. As time passed, I found myself more comfortable opening up and being vulnerable in front of others. At each event, I played the slideshow, shared my story, and then joined the participants in sweating through that long workout. Afterwards, people would inevitably approach me with that blank look in their eyes, a stare I knew all too well. And then they would tell me of their own shadow, their own horror. Oftentimes they would thank me for being willing to share my story, saying that it gave them the courage to share theirs. I never felt like I was doing anything special or particularly brave, I just knew that if my imperfect story could somehow help someone else, it was worth standing in front of a room and telling it. As the years passed, I took great joy in seeing the very people who first approached me with that blank stare in their eyes now smiling and full of life. Another person who didn't have to live in the shadows.

At one particular event, I stood up to share my story, and as I talked I looked around to see the faces of dozens of engaged listeners. All except for one. Near the back stood a stout and muscular man with an expression that read, "Don't mess with me or I'll kick your ass." I moved on and didn't think much of it. But as I talked more, I noticed him again, standing in the back with that same look on his face. The time came for the workout to begin. I dove right in, sweating profusely within minutes. A few rounds into the WOD, I heard a voice behind me yell, "Come on man, fight through it!" I turned to see the same man who had been standing in the back. I continued the workout, round after round. Then I heard the voice again, "Where are you at?"

"I'm finishing round seven," I answered.

"Well, don't let me catch you," he said sternly. I finished my eighth round and headed out for the 800 meter run to the sound of his yells, pushing me to finish strong.

A few minutes later, as I stood off to the side of the gym, shirtless and double-fisting a couple of cold beers, the same man walked toward me, that familiar blank stare in his eyes. Suddenly his head was buried in my chest, tears streaming down his face. Given his tough demeanor, the open display of emotion surprised me. But sometimes the softest hearts lie behind the hardest walls. I pulled my arms around him, letting him cry against me.

After a few moments, he straightened up, wiping his eyes and drawing breaths to compose himself. "You know, I almost didn't come today," he said. "A few months ago, my dad was diagnosed with cancer. And since then, I've just been pissed off at the world. I've been asking myself, 'Why me? Why us?' It just seems so unfair. But what I realized, through listening to you today, is that I can't change the fact that my dad has cancer, but I have an opportunity that the families of the men you shared about today didn't have. I get to take a victory lap with my old man. And you know what? I'm going to do it."

He thanked me for what I shared and finished with, "Keep doing what you're doing. You never know when someone like me needs to hear exactly what you have to say." He sent me a friend request on social media that day, one that I quickly accepted. Over the next few months, I had the privilege of watching him take a victory lap with his dad. Every few weeks a picture would pop up on my newsfeed of him and his dad, side-by-side and smiling, while checking off another item from the bucket list, treasuring the last few months they had together. Each post finished with #victorylap #legion8. And then one day I opened up my

Facebook account to see a post informing us that his father had passed away. In the post, he talked about the fact that although he was sad, he wouldn't trade those last months he got to spend with his dad for anything. He wrote how he would see his father again and they would finally finish what they started. Seeing things like this reminded me once again that when you make the choice to use what you have been through for good, nothing is wasted. The pain, the seemingly senseless deaths, the darkness, it was now a force for good.

I remained in contact with most of the families of the Legion 8 men. While still in Iraq, I had been able to get in touch with PFC James Arnold's sister, Christie. We connected and agreed to stay in touch. But when I tried to make contact again, months later when I returned, I realized that she had changed her email address, leaving me no way to connect with her or her family. I searched for a way to make contact, but all of my efforts came up empty. As Legion 8 continued to grow, I wanted to find a way more than ever to contact PFC Arnold's family to share with them about what we were doing. So I continued to scour the internet for anything that might help me find them. One day, while searching online, I came across a picture of a jersey hung in a coffee shop, in honor of no other than PFC James Arnold. I tracked down the name of the coffee shop, found a phone number, and called. When a woman on the other end answered the phone I said, "This might be one of the strangest calls you'll ever receive, but I was wondering if you could help me out with something."

I went on to explain who I was and how I was trying to find a way to get in touch with Arnold's family. The woman was quite moved by the story and happy to help. Through that connection, I was able to get in touch with another one of Arnold's sisters, Amanda. We talked a bit and even had dinner in Minnesota, where she lived. I still carried a deep weight of guilt every time I thought of the fact that my choice to switch places with Arnold resulted in the death of such a good man. What would his family think if they knew?

A few years later, in 2015, the whole Arnold family traveled down to Tyler to attend one of the Legion 8 events at Premier CrossFit. I looked over to see Arnold's mom sitting down, watching as people filed into the room. I knew I had to talk with her. I knew what I had to say. I asked to speak with her privately and she stood and walked with me, away from the busy throng of people working to get everything set up and ready to begin the event.

"Before we begin, there's something I need to tell you," I said. "I don't know if you know this already, but…." And that was all I could get out. The words caught in my throat, choked by emotion. I looked into her eyes, the eyes of a mother who would never again see her son because of one small decision that I made. It shouldn't have been him; it should have been me. Tears streamed down my face. I tried again to speak the words, the confession of the truth that she had to know. But I couldn't. No words came out, only tears. She grabbed me and pulled me against her chest. She hugged me and held me, as if I was her own son.

"I know what you're going to tell me," she said. "I already know. I know you switched seats with my Jimmy, But you know what? That just tells me that God was ready for Jimmy, and he's not ready for you yet. He needs you here to carry on with what you're doing and make sure that everyone remembers our boys, and He needs Jimmy up there for a reason that I don't know yet. But I know that when I join my Jimmy someday, it will all make sense." Her words poured over me like ointment, healing a wound that had festered for years.

People told me that I was brave and strong to have the courage to stand up and tell my story, but that was nothing compared to the sheer will of that woman, that mother, to choose to somehow see the good amidst her greatest pain. Her courage, her love, her unwavering stand against the bitterness that was rightfully hers to harbor, will forever be one of the most inspiring things I have ever witnessed.

That night we had a party. The Arnold family, Lynda Kagan, and several others who were connected to the Legion 8 men, as well as a handful of my friends and fellow CrossFitters, all gathered together that night. We laughed, we drank, we ate, and we talked. As the hour grew late, Lynda stood, emboldened by a few choice drinks, and called for everyone's attention. The small kitchen where we congregated grew silent. "You know, I do a lot of work with Gold Star parents," she began, referring to parents of U.S. Armed Forces members who have died in service to the country. "Recently, I mentioned Legion 8 to another Gold Star mom. I told her what we are doing and how much it's grown. When I finished talking, I looked into the eyes of that woman and all I saw was sadness. I asked her what was wrong and she simply said, 'My boy doesn't have a Legion 8.' Her words just hit home with me. We can't ever take what we have, this community, this love for granted. So I want to take a moment to honor Jeff and recognize that we wouldn't all be here if it weren't for him. Jeff, I know I've said it before, but I want to say it publicly... I love you, we all love you. And we are all so grateful for what you've done."

Her words once again solidified in me the resolution to use my life and my story for good. If all of the effort and all of the time was just to make a difference in that one woman's life, it would be worth it. Legion 8 began with the desire to honor eight incredible men who died, a desire that will always be the cornerstone of its identity. But it grew into so much more, a fact that would undoubtedly make each of those eight men proud.

After years of sharing my story and having people share theirs with me, stories of sexual assault, losing a loved one, or experiencing another traumatic event, I realized that pain, grief, and what many refer to as "Post-Traumatic Stress Disorder" is not at all exclusive to the military. A buddy of mine, Josh Mantz, coined the term "Moral Casualty," a fitting description for many who have gone through trauma. People know how to treat broken bones, but how do you treat moral casualties? What about the scars and wounds on our hearts and minds? No one feels shame from a broken leg or the need to hide a wounded arm, and yet all of us feel the need to cover up our emotional brokenness. So many people are afraid to share what they've been through. I know I was. I thought people would avoid me and treat me differently, I thought it would change everything. But when I made the choice to step out, to live in the light, I found out just how wrong I was.

Sometimes it just takes one person in a room who is willing to be the first to raise a hand, to reveal scars, to share a story. Sometimes it's that one single act that creates a safe space for others to do the same. Legion has transcended beyond one unit of incredible men that I had the pleasure of serving with. It now encompasses those who have fought and are fighting to awaken, heal, and recover from trauma or challenging circumstances. It's the woman who is still haunted by the memory of being raped as a teenager. It's the man grappling with the sudden loss of his father. It's the mother's tears that drip onto the tombstone of her son. It's the war veteran, the widow, the abuse victim, the recovery addict. We are Legion.

And together, we will rise.

Epilogue

"It is not the critic who counts; not the man who points out how the strong man stumbles, or where the doer of deeds could have done them better. The credit belongs to the man who is actually in the arena, whose face is marred by dust and sweat and blood; who strives valiantly; who errs, who comes short again and again, because there is no effort without error and shortcoming; but who does actually strive to do the deeds; who knows great enthusiasms, the great devotions; who spends himself in a worthy cause; who at the best knows in the end the triumph of high achievement, and who at the worst, if he fails, at least fails while daring greatly, so that his place shall never be with those cold and timid souls who neither know victory nor defeat."—Theodore Roosevelt

Present day.

I wake up before the first hints of sunlight. Rising out of bed, I'm careful not to wake the beautiful sleeping woman beside me, her long brown hair falling over her pillow, eyes closed, breathing deeply. My wife, Anne. The one who embraces all of me, who supports me, who not only allows but encourages me to continue being the best I can be. She entered my life just as I began to reawaken, bringing a particular kind of light and love into my world that I soon realized I couldn't live without. She is strong, kind, and readily makes sacrifices on my behalf, understanding that my experiences, the men I served with, and the duty to use my story for good are things that will always be a part of me.

I walk quietly through the house, mindful of our young children sleeping in their beds—Will, Jack, and our newborn baby girl, Claire. As my good friend Rich Harkins always says, "When it comes to raising children, the days are long but the years are short." I have seen the truth in those words as I have watched Cole grow into the fine young man he is today. And I know that, in less than a blink of an eye, my young children will also grow into ambitious young men and women, ready to take on the world just as I once was.

I go for a run, my pumping heart and burning lungs awakening my senses to the new day ahead. A cup of steaming coffee awaits me at the end, and I pour myself a generous mugful while catching my breath. And then I walk outside and take my seat to watch the sun rise.

In these moments as I await the day ahead, I am quiet and still, alone with my thoughts.

And I think.

I think about acceptance, often. And about opportunity. And I think about the power of choice.

There are things that have happened in my life that I wish hadn't. Things I didn't choose. Things I had no control over. And I know I'm not alone in feeling that way. All of us are forced to walk through situations that we wish we didn't have to. All of us have pain, loss, and grief that we desperately wish we could disown. Sometimes life gives you things that you didn't ask for, things you don't want, things that you want to push away, give back, refuse to accept.

No one asks to lose eight good men under their leadership. No one asks to hold the shattered face of a heroic young man and listen to the sound of his agony as he dies. No one asks for their son to be killed on a lonely Iraqi road. No one asks for their father to be diagnosed with cancer. No one asks to be raped or abused. No one asks for a loved one to die. These are our shadows, shadows we didn't ask for, that follow us no matter how many times we try to shake them.

And in the face of our pain, a natural desire in all of us arises—the desire to fight. And so we fight. *I didn't ask for this. I don't want this. I can't accept this.* We shout these sentiments, refusing to allow the painful experiences to become part of who we are. But every time we fight, every time we stand up and refuse to accept the things that have happened to us, we are knocked back down with the reality that we are fighting something that just... *is.* Something that can't be changed. Something that will forever be there, will always be true. When we fight the shadows, they will always emerge the victor, and we find ourselves rendered the victim, defeated once again. This is a vicious cycle that holds us prisoner and, over time, begins to define us. Fighting the parts of our stories that we wish we could change, and desperately trying to erase the things that haunt us, will only result in us feeling powerless and paralyzed.

But when we face the shadow and we walk straight through it, straight into true acceptance that it will always be a part of us, we abolish the control it holds over us. And then, then we emerge, holding in our hands the power to choose what comes next, to choose what we will do with this life that is ours. I believe the power of choice is truly the single greatest gift we, as humans, are given.

We can't change the things that we have seen or the experiences we have been through. They will always be with us, always be part of us—placing on our shoulders both a burden and a privilege to bear. But each day we have an opportunity: to look ourselves squarely in the mirror, to accept the entirety of who we are, and to choose to use all of it for good.

This cannot be accomplished through a single choice that forever changes everything. No, this is a choice we must make daily—to rise up and decide to do something with the life we've been given. We won't always do it perfectly. Sometimes we will falter and fail. But with each new morning, we have the opportunity to make the choice once again.

So here I sit, watching the sun rise for a new day, and I ask myself...

"What's it going to be today, Jeff?"

Note From L.C. Mickler/ Letters

Note from L.C. Mickler:

The first time Jeff and I sat down to discuss writing his story, he was emphatic about one thing: he wanted this story to be truthful, raw, and authentic. He didn't want to sugarcoat his experiences and he didn't want to be painted with a brush that only depicted him in the best of light. He wanted the entirety of his story and his character to be portrayed...the good, the noble, the ugly, the human. And so we agreed that, together, we would strive to create an honest narrative, one that captures all aspects of the man Jeff is.

Through the entire writing process, Jeff never once shied away from telling his story with courageous honesty, even when it was hard. But as we finished the manuscript, I felt that something was missing. In order to fulfill the promise that we made, I felt it necessary to bring to light the great impact he has made in the lives of so many people. The book alludes to his connection with others, but I knew that we needed something more to adequately illustrate the man that he is. Being a strong leader and devoting his life to helping others is truly integral to his character. So I took it upon myself to contact a small handful of people that have been in some way changed by Jeff's life and story, and I asked them to share a brief glimpse of how they have been touched by him. Each person I contacted was eager to participate.

So here it is, the last paintbrush, the final strokes, in the simple words of those who have been impacted by him the most.

—L.C. Mickler

Written by Lynda Kagan, mother of SGT Ryan Green:

You have asked me to talk about Capt. Jeff... and yes, to me he will always be Capt. Jeff (although he hates that).

To explain our relationship is hard, not just because it came about because of terrible circumstances but because it's hard to put into words how deeply I feel for this man.

Jeff was my son's captain. And Ryan is one of the Legion 8 men.

I never met Jeff prior to Ryan's death. I met him only when he called from Iraq and put the phone up to my Ryan's ear so I could talk to him one last time. To be honest, I didn't remember that until many years after Ryan passed.

Jeff is a man of honor; every promise that he has ever made he has kept. It would have been easy to walk away from us, but he didn't. He made it a point to come visit us when he returned to the states. There are not many who do this, but he did. More than that, he welcomed our questions…how hard that must have been. My husband, Craig, was always respectful with his questions, but I always pushed for more. It used to irritate Craig, but I had to know what happened. Capt. Jeff never wavered. Somehow he understood my need to know. And he went above and beyond to make sure I had the answers and information I needed. He understood this Mama's heart.

Two years after Ryan was killed in Iraq, my Craig died from cancer. I was alone. But I wasn't. I had my family and my boys.

If you had asked me on that day in March of 2007 if I would have the relationships I have now, I would have told you no.

What Jeff did in his tenure with the 1/8 was to establish a family. The mentality of that group of men to include us, to love us, to embrace us as family is incredible. It is truly exceptional.

True leaders lead. Jeff Morris is a leader with a pure heart. I am proud to know him and proud to call him my son (albeit from another mother).

Written by Doug Walker:

I have had the pleasure of knowing Jeff for many years, and I have the honor of calling him a friend. I met Jeff at a mutual friend's birthday party. My friend mentioned that he had gone to college with Jeff and had known him for quite some time. Because of our affinity for CrossFit and because of our mutual friend, our paths started to cross more and more often. Then, Jeff joined the CrossFit gym I had been attending for many years. We began to work out together, have lots of laughs, and push each other in the workouts. Jeff is an excellent CrossFitter and a great athlete in general. Our friendship grew, and I begin to know Jeff on a more personal level. One thing that was very apparent early on was that Jeff is a person of substance. As we began to learn more and more about each other, I was made aware of his military service. One day, Jeff told me about Legion 8 and the workout dedicated to the fallen heroes. The story was unlike anything I had every heard. I have always been a big fan of the men and women that serve our country, but this story moved me deeply.

Jeff was planning to do a Legion 8 event in Tyler, Texas. He made me aware of it and I told him I would be there. To be honest, I don't think he believed that I would travel a couple of hours each way and spend the night to make the event. When I walked in the door with my wife and mutual friends, Jeff's face lit up. He started telling me how much he appreciated it and was going on a bit. I interrupted him and said, "You are my friend, I love you and I am here to support you." That was just the thought that was on my mind at the moment, and it was from the heart.

Since that time, we have hung out, I have visited him when Anne gave birth to their son, and we have been a part of an "infamous" texting group with me, Jeff, and our friend Donnie.

On September 1st, 2017, my 16-year-old daughter, Caroline Walker, was killed in an accident. She was smart, funny, likable, unselfish, and lit up every room she ever entered. Needless to say, this has been the greatest struggle in my life. I deal with grief on a daily basis. The only reason I am able to get out of bed is because of my faith in God, family, and my beloved friends.

We had a memorial service for Caroline about one week after she passed away. After the service, we had a celebration of life party at our house. As it got close to midnight, just a few of us guys were hanging out on my patio, talking and smoking cigars. When almost everyone had left, Jeff asked if he could speak to me in private. He began to tell me in more detail than ever before about the grief and guilt he experienced after his soldiers died in battle. He said that he lost a few years due to not facing things head on and not dealing with things on many levels. He told me that Caroline's death was my destiny, whether I liked it or not. Whether I wanted to accept it or not. He encouraged me to embrace reality and not just survive, but thrive.

Since that party, I have read eight books and watched numerous sermons and videos on grief. To this day, Jeff's advice has been the best and most impactful advice I have received about accepting my fate and moving on. A few months later, Jeff said he wanted to do a Legion 8 workout at my CrossFit gym, but the theme would be centered around Caroline. I am a good public speaker and I have heard many, many speeches, but Jeff's speech that day was one of the best I have ever witnessed. In his speech, he told the story about me going to Tyler for the Legion 8 event and told everyone that I said, "You are my friend, I love you, and I am here to support you." As he said it, his voice cracked and he turned away from the audience to get his composure. I had long since forgotten I had said that and I had no idea it meant so much to him. After he was done speaking, I hugged him and said, "I love you with all my heart." It is a moment I will cherish for the rest of my life. Jeff has always been a good friend, but we became brothers that day.

Written by Amanda Arnold, sister of PFC James L. Arnold:

I'll never forget the day I spoke to a complete stranger by the name of Jeff Morris. Little did I know that he would not only end up becoming my friend, but also truly embody what I consider a true hero. In fact, he changed my life.

It was 2013 and I was living in Phoenix on my own—part of my newly developed "adventurous" side since my brother's passing six years earlier. Jeff left me a voicemail message, and as I listened to it for once I actually felt compelled to speak to the person on the other end, despite the fact that it was a complete stranger. I can remember exactly where I was standing in my kitchen when I actually spoke with Jeff for the first time, the man who said he was Jimmy's commanding officer while in Iraq. I never personally met the men from Legion that my brother claimed as brothers and friends. He was the only boy (and the baby) among four sisters. Regrettably, I never went to visit him while stationed at boot camp or Fort Hood because I always assumed there would be a next time.

Jeff explained to me that he had tried for a long time to find my family, eventually reaching out to a local coffee shop in our small hometown and leaving his contact info for the owners to send to my dad. I couldn't believe that someone would go to such lengths for so long, but I'm glad he did.

After some small talk, he asked me if I wanted to know about that day, the day my brother was killed. When I said yes, he told me about it all, sharing all of the details of what happened, details that I still censor to my own mother. I wrote down everything he said so I would not forget the events that occurred and the emotions it made me feel.

Ultimately, Jeff told me he ordered Jimmy to take his spot in the Humvee that day. Jeff said that Jimmy was not supposed to be in that seat, that he should have been the one in it. My reply was, "God has bigger plans for you, Jeff." I'm no saint, sometimes I still try to get angry over it, but I cannot. Jeff has made too much of an impact to my life to get angry at him.

Spiritual or not, you have to admire the courage of a man like Jeff Morris. To track a family member down after so many years and to be able to share those intimate details without knowing what the reaction could be takes a tremendous amount of courage. I could only wish for it. Those moments had an ever-changing impact on my life and the emotions are something I cannot share in writing, but I will always remember.

Several months later, after I moved to Minneapolis, we finally met. We laughed, we cried, we talked about life. He told me things about his time in Iraq, the things he experienced, and his journey being back home. I cannot imagine the struggles he personally faced and yet all he cared about was remembering his guys—his friends and brothers. I couldn't get over how often he checked in on me, making sure my family and I were okay. Who does that? The work he is doing with Legion 8, remembering the men and bringing strangers together for a good cause, causes me to often ask myself what I can do to be a fraction of the person Jeff Morris is. He introduced me to the parents, spouses, and friends of the Legion 8 men—people that will always have a place in my heart now, regardless of how often we talk. I've cried with the parents of Green and Prater and the widow of Harris. I've had beers amongst the men who served with my brother. Because of Jeff Morris, these people are a part of my life and because of Jeff Morris, those fallen live on forever in our hearts and our memories. We are not alone in mourning their loss, but rather, we have a life-long bond.

I've never been good with words, but I've tried to tell Jeff several times what an impact he's had on my life, my family's, and anyone else's life he's likely ever talked to. I also struggle being able to convey to others the impact he's had on my life. It brings me so much joy to see him as a dad, a husband, a confidant, a best friend, a leader, and much more. It brings peace to my heart to see that he's not wasting away a chance at life, but doing the complete opposite. God truly did have bigger plans for Jeff that day, and I can't thank him enough for everything he's done and continues to do for everyone else. He truly is a hero in my eyes…in more ways than I can express.

For More News About Jeff Morris or L.C. Mickler, Signup For Our Newsletter:

http://wbp.bz/newsletter

Word-of-mouth is critical to an author's long-term success. If you appreciated this book please leave a review on the Amazon sales page:

http://wbp.bz/legionrisinga

AVAILABLE FROM CRAIG DRUMMOND AND WILDBLUE PRESS!

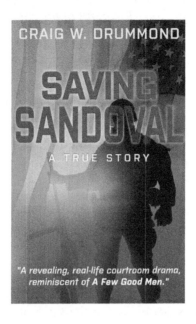

SAVING SANDOVAL by CRAIG W. DRUMMOND

http://wbp.bz/savingsandovala

Read A Sample Next

ONE – THE ARREST

"The sniper must be able to calmly and deliberately kill targets that may not pose an immediate threat to him. It is much easier to kill in self-defense or in the defense of others than it is to kill without apparent provocation."

~ *"Sniper Training," U.S. Army Field Manual 23-10 (1994)*

On 26 June 2007, two United States Army Criminal Investigation Command (CID) Agents quietly approached the front door of a home in Laredo, Texas, and knocked. Their mission: to arrest U.S. Army sniper, Specialist Jorge Sandoval, Jr.

Specialist Sandoval recalled in a 2016 interview:

"It was only a few days after my twenty-second birthday when the agents showed up. I was home on leave from Iraq and excited to be home to spend my birthday with my family. I was at my mom's house, doing some push-ups and working out. Mom was in the kitchen making lunch. It surprised me to hear a knock on the door because I hadn't heard any vehicles approaching the house.

I answered the door and was greeted by two gentlemen wearing polo shirts and cargo pants. They identified themselves as Army CID Agents and asked me, "Are you Specialist Jorge Sandoval, Jr.?"

"Yes." I said, "What is this about?" I stepped outside and that's when I saw two vehicles—an unmarked vehicle and a police vehicle with lights flashing.

"We need to ask you some questions related to an incident that occurred while you were in Iraq. We will need you to accompany us to the police station for questioning."

"Fine. Just let me go inside and get dressed," I said.

I quickly changed my clothes, and when my mom saw that I had changed, she asked me where I was going. *"Adonde vas, mijo?"*

I responded in Spanish, saying, "Look, I don't know... some people want to talk to me. I don't know what it's about. When I find out what's going on, I'll let you know... but I must tell you, I don't know if I'm coming back.'

As the agents were escorting me away from the house I thought, *Maybe something happened with one of my friends in Iraq.* I assumed I was getting into their unmarked vehicle with them so I began to move toward the car door to open it.

"No," they said, stopping me. "You're not going to ride in this vehicle."

Two local police officers blocked off both sides of the road, put my hands behind my back, put me in handcuffs, and put me into the back of a squad car.

That was the moment I first started to realize that I was in some type of custody. *Okay, so this definitely has something to do with me,* I thought, *not one of my friends. What could have happened? Why am I being taken into custody? Did I do something wrong?*

As I tried to get a grasp of the situation, all sorts of things were going through my mind. I traveled back in my memory to Iraq, quickly flipping through my recollections of various dates, trying to get a sense of what was happening to me. I thought back to the events that led to me and a few friends of mine finding ourselves in sniper positions in the U.S. Army.

As the squad car pulled away from my mom's house with me inside, I thought, *This is terrible timing! Michelle's waiting for me, and she's going to think I stood her up.* Michelle was a childhood friend and we had just recently reconnected and started dating. I knew I couldn't text her from the squad car.

When we got to the police station, I was put in an interrogation room and my phone was placed on the table in front of me. It immediately started ringing. I knew it was Michelle.

For two hours, an interrogation was conducted by one of the CID Agents who had come to my mother's door and a female agent who had stayed in the unmarked vehicle as I was being picked up. They interrogated me about missions I had undertaken in Iraq during April and May of 2007. The phone continued to ring and ring, but I was forbidden to answer it.

I tried to answer their questions to the fullest of my ability. At no point during the interrogation did they reveal to me why I was being held and questioned. Finally, their questioning started to wind down, so I asked, "Am I free to go? Can I leave now? And, can I please have my phone back?'

The two agents glanced at each other and then one of them said, "No, son. You're going back to the theater." (2)

"Back to the theater?" Back to Iraq? I couldn't believe they were sending me back to the Middle East.

"Okaaaayyy…" I said, still in the dark as to what was going on.

One of them handed me back my phone. "I am giving you one call. I recommend you call your parents. Have them pack a bag for you and meet you here."

I had been handcuffed, taken to the police station in a squad car, interrogated, and had my phone taken away. Now I was being sent back to the theater. By this point, I had put two

---

2   Theater is the term used to describe a "theater of war" or "theater of operations" and can encompass an entire area of armed conflict including actual battlefields and surrounding area; for example, Iraq.

and two together. *They're not sending me back to fight. I'm going to be spending time in prison somewhere.*

"Listen," I told my mother in Spanish when I got her on the phone, "you need to pack a bag for me. Can you grab my assault backpack—the pack that looks like it's from the Army? Put everything that looks like it's from the Army in there and bring it to me at the police station."

When I was taken out to the main entrance of the police station to wait for my mom to arrive with my pack, I was surprised to see my entire family waiting there to say goodbye to me. They all had very serious expressions on their faces.

My mother must have hung up with me and then quickly called my father. (They had been separated since I was four years old.) She must have also called my two sisters. I hated for them to see me in that situation, but I was grateful for the chance to say goodbye.

"Say your goodbyes quickly," the agents told me. They gave me the feeling that I was going away and not coming back.

My family asked me in Spanish what was going on. I told them, "These people are from the military. There's something going on..."

Before saying goodbye to my family, I had been shown the charge sheet from my Army commander so I knew exactly what was going on. The charge sheet stated:

Charge I: Violation of the UCMJ, Article 118... The Specification: In that Specialist Jorge G. Sandoval, Jr., did, at or near Abu Shemsi, Iraq, on or about 27 April, 2007, murder an Iraqi national by means of shooting him with a rifle.

***Charge II: Violation of the UCMJ, Article 134... The
Specification:*** *In that Specialist Jorge G. Sandoval, Jr., did,
at or near Jurf as Sakhr, Iraq, on or about 11 May, 2007,
wrongfully place command wire(3) with the remains of
Genei Nesir Khudair Al-Janabi, which conduct was to the
prejudice of good order and discipline in the armed forces
or of a nature to bring discredit upon the armed forces.*

◆ ◆ ◆

I recalled doing my final preparations for the 27 April 2007
mission. Although I had been on missions before, it was
going to be my first or second mission as a sniper, and I had
the nervous feeling everyone gets in advance of a mission.
As we moved closer to the start time of that mission, I felt
the nerves and jitters and tried to consider all the possibilities
and anticipate what could happen. From the time you
actually leave the gate of the base, you put all that aside and
focus on your mission and your objectives.

I believe that Sergeant Hensley and I took off around one in
the morning, and then the rest of the team took off twenty or
thirty minutes behind us. Since I had gone on the initial recon
of the area, Sergeant Hensley made me the point person of
our team. I felt confident with GPS and knew where we were
going and what we were doing.

---

3   Command wire is normal electrical wire but is commonly
used by insurgents in rigging improvised explosive devices
(IEDs) and other types of bombs to attack U.S. and coalition
forces.

Sergeant Hensley and I understood each other. We knew what to do. From the time we received the warning order(4), we already knew what to ask and what to do when it came to packing. Based on how many days we'd be gone, we knew how much water we would need because we had learned from other missions where we ran out of water or food. We were past that stage where we needed other people to look after us.

Our mission was to interdict the mortar team attacking friendly units in our area of responsibility. I felt confident up until we made it to a certain point where we hadn't yet done recon in the area. So, we got to this one area and I remember there being this good-sized canal filled with water. We couldn't seem to find a way across it but we had to continue our mission and get to our objective regardless.

Sergeant Hensley found what looked like a good spot to cross and said, "Oh, hey, we could cross it right through here." "Okay, I said, "Sounds good."

In the dark of the early morning, Sergeant Hensley went into the canal before me, carrying his assault pack with his sustainment for the seventy-two-hour mission. I was carrying a rucksack with a ton of water along with our mission equipment radios and a bunch of other stuff. You waterproof everything as much as you can, but there's only so much you can do.

---

4   A warning order, or WARNO, is the term for an order issued by the military command concerning an upcoming mission. A warning order is normally general in nature and issued as soon as possible to give the date, time, and known information about the mission so that preparations can begin. A warning order is normally followed by a formal operations order providing specific details concerning the mission.

I pulled security as Sergeant Hensley crossed.

"Oh, man, this canal is so deep!" he said.

He is six-foot-three or four, so the water only came up to his upper chest and neck area. Watching him and knowing I'm only five-foot-eight, I thought, *Crossing this is going to suck for me!*

Sure enough, I was completely submerged from head to toe. The only thing I was able to keep above my head was my rifle. Everything else went into the canal with me. When I finally reached the other side of the canal, I threw my rifle up on the bank and came up with my hand sticking out. I assumed Sergeant Hensley would give me a hand, but he was so focused on the mission that once he saw that I was almost out of the canal, he turned and started walking.

At the time I thought, *What the hell?!* But I knew why he kept going. He was just focused on the mission. The two of us understood each other. Not just the two of us—the sniper section in general.

I managed to grab hold of some tall vegetation on the bank and pull myself out, but I lost so much energy, it took a while to regain my bearings. As soon as I was out of the canal, I saw a house and heard some dogs barking. *This is not good,* I said to myself.

I looked through my night vision goggles and there was Sergeant Hensley about fifty meters away, still walking. Since he hadn't waited for me or stuck around to make sure I'd made it out of the canal without drowning, I had no other choice but to catch up.

We reached the rendezvous rally point where we were supposed to meet the other team that had set out twenty minutes after us. Once they showed up, I noticed they were totally dry, head to toe. They had found a crossing further up the canal and crossed there. I couldn't believe it.

We all sat together for three to five minutes, made a map check, and sent up our present position to let higher command know we were moving on to our objective overwatch. All the while, I was still trying to get my breath back from the canal crossing. I had damn near drowned and was exhausted. Then about another 200 meters into our movement, I rolled my ankle. It was only the first night of a seventy-two-hour mission and already I'd nearly drowned and rolled my ankle. My ankle had been bad from the start as I broke it in high school, and it never fully healed.

What kept going through my head was the fact that I'd heard dogs barking when I got out of the canal. All I could think was, *Hopefully we won't get attacked!*

Sergeant Hensley and I separated from the others. I believe two other sniper teams with .50 caliber sniper rifles went off to their own hide-site(5) and me and Hensley continued on our way to ours. Every step I took a step on my badly swollen ankle was agonizing. Once at the hide-site, I threw myself on my rucksack and leaned back on it. I left my boot on as I knew that if I took it off, my ankle would be in worse shape.

It was all business from there. Security was us, just him and me. We set up a sleep plan where we would sleep in one-hour shifts, one hour up and one hour down.

We stood up, surveyed the area, looked around, and then went into our sleep plan. We had already set up all our communications. We were lying down on our stomachs doing our mission and I thought, *As long as we don't do*

---

5   The location where sniper teams, or other light infantry units, consolidate to rest, pull security and/or fire at the enemy is termed a hide-site, as it is the location where they are hiding.

anything and I don't have to move my ankle too much, the swelling will go down.

We had gotten to our objective around three o'clock that morning, and sunrise would come around six. We were still in our rest plan. We had gotten off to a rough start, but now Sergeant Hensley and I were talking and hanging out, passing the time.

Right around sunrise, we were in our hide-site—a small dry canal—sitting up under a bushy tree. We both heard voices in the area and looked at each other and knew that we were thinking the same thing: "Oh, shit! Somebody's coming!"

We didn't want to pop up and get compromised only hours into our mission. We saw three individuals pass right by the canal. They just walked right by. We didn't think they saw us, so we left it at that. They were males, not that old, maybe in their twenties.

I knew that whatever happened, I could trust Sergeant Hensley. We totally understood each other. And we knew what to do.

♦ ♦ ♦

As I was saying goodbye to my family, I told them, "I want you to hear this from me before you hear it from anyone else. I am being charged with the murder of an Iraqi man. I just want you to know that I was just doing my job. That's it. Everything's going to be fine."

I kissed my mom on the cheek. *"Te quiero mucho, Mamma. Nos vemos pronto."*(6)

When I told my family that everything was going to be fine, I didn't necessarily believe it myself. I just wanted to comfort them.

---

6   "I love you so much Mamma, see you soon."

As the CID Agents transported me, I wanted to object and say, "What do you mean you're sending me back to the theater? I've only used up ten of my fifteen days of leave time!"

I knew there was no point. They weren't treating me disrespectfully, but they were definitely treating me as if I had already been convicted of murder.

http://wbp.bz/savingsandovala

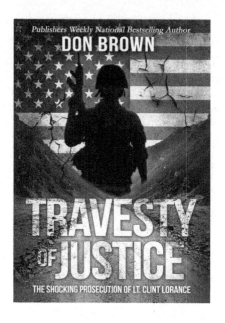
Introduction

Landmines,

Suicide Bikers

and the Bloody War in Afghanistan

On July 2, 2012, two days before Independence Day in America, a young Army lieutenant, a decorated member of the elite 82nd Airborne Division, took charge of his platoon in Kandahar Province, Afghanistan. First Lieutenant Clint Lorance was one of the most decorated junior officers in the United States Army.

With an impressive seven Army Achievement Medals on his chest, most of them earned as an enlisted man, Clint had served overseas on two separate tours before Afghanistan. First, he was assigned to the Eighth Army in Korea in Pusan, where he was often near the dangerous and volatile Demilitarized Zone on the border between North and South Korea. After that, he served in Iraq, during the Iraq War, at Forward Operating Base Kalsu, 20 miles south of Baghdad. During his tour in Iraq, Clint's post came under heavy rocket and mortar fire from the enemy on a daily basis. He often led dangerous convoys outside of the post while in Iraq, frequently drawing rocket fire, mortar fire, and gunfire.

Clint put his life on the line for his country. Many soldiers, coming under the type of constant fire that Clint had endured in Iraq, elected to do their time and get out. That is understandable. Combat is a living hell that most Americans will never be forced to witness up close and personal. For those who served and then got out, their service is no less diminished, and should be greatly appreciated by all Americans.

At the end of his dangerous tour in Iraq, Clint could have left the Army. A number of his buddies did. But Clint elected to stay. Service to his country was in his bloodstream and ran through his veins. Clint Lorance wanted to continue to serve, even if it meant giving his life for America.

The Army recognized his hard work, dedication, and service to his country, and offered him the opportunity to earn a commission as an officer. He responded to the challenge, and entered the Army's Green-to-Gold program, competing to become an officer in the United States Army. Clint excelled in the officer candidate program, soon earned his commission as a second lieutenant in the infantry, and then became a paratrooper in the elite 82nd Airborne Division.

Now, as a young officer, he had been called to serve his country in a third dangerous overseas tour, this time in Afghanistan.

On the morning of July 2nd, Clint had been on the job as platoon leader for only three days when he called his men together at 5:55 a.m. to brief them on the day's mission.

Lorance had been called in to take command of First Platoon, Charlie Company, when the platoon's previous commander, First Lieutenant Dom Latino, was wounded by an exploding improvised exploding device (IED), which blew the hell up when another American soldier stepped on it, a couple of weeks before Clint Lorance would take command. Shrapnel had torn through Latino's face and abdomen, and they rushed him off the battlefield to try and save his life. Like Latino, many of the soldiers in First Platoon had taken a beating from the IEDs. Some were injured, some maimed, others killed.

An IED is a deadly, homemade bomb built by the Taliban, and then hidden in the ground, for the purpose of killing and maiming American soldiers. Between 2008 and 2010, nearly 60 percent of American soldiers who died in Afghanistan were killed by IEDs. Sometimes, these devices were set off remotely, triggered via radio transmitters in the hands of Taliban operatives hiding well out of sight.

Sometimes, a single step on a routine patrol triggered the explosion, as these "pressure plate IEDs" were set off by pressure alone. But whether the IEDs were pressure detonated, or radio triggered, the results proved deadly for American GIs.

In southeastern Afghanistan, where Clint and his men had been deployed, the environment was exceptionally dangerous.

Here's what 4th Brigade Deputy Brigade Commander Col. Scott Halstead, who later testified in the court-martial of Lieutenant Lorance, said, under oath, at trial, about the battlefield conditions in which these paratroopers were operating:

"Zhari/Maiwand (the district in Kandahar province where the platoon operated) is almost entirely—I mean it's a gigantic minefield ... Our paratroopers were, justifiably so, very cautious. They'd seen many of their Ranger buddies killed and maimed."

In addition to mine-ridden battlefields, the Taliban had been employing another terror tactic to kill Americans. A tactic that was impossible to defend against.

Motorcycles.

The Taliban had begun strapping explosives to their bodies, mounting motorcycles, and then charging toward American troops, blowing themselves up at close range. This became known as a "VBIED attack" for Vehicle Borne Improvised Explosive Device. This tactic gave attackers the dual advantage of 1) engaging in Islamic martyrdom, while 2) murdering Americans and anyone who sympathized with Americans. The tactic of mass-murder-by-motorcycle had increased in recent months, and under suicidal rules of engagement employed by the American military in 2012, self-defense against suicide bikers became an impossible choice.

American troops were hand-strapped from firing, unless they could first determine "hostile intent," which normally meant identifying a weapon on the attacker. Then, after determining the presence of "hostile intent," our soldiers had to analyze the enemy for a potential "hostile act."

The American soldier in 2012 was relegated to the role of battlefield lawyer, forced into a series of mental gymnastics to reach a legal conclusion about whether to fire in self-defense. All this in a war-torn battle zone, in a historically war-torn country, in the ancestral home of the Taliban.

But the Americans could not always identify bombs on fast-approaching motorcycles. Nor could they see bombs under the insurgent's shirt, or hidden within the motorcycle. Motorcycles moved too quickly for positive identification of anything, and life or death often hung upon split-second decisions.

Soldiers were trained to fight, not to play lawyer on the battlefield.

A split-second too long of playing lawyer in a barbaric war zone, then deciding at the last second to refrain from firing against a fast-charging motorcycle, could lead to instant carnage, perhaps multiple deaths for American troops in the motorcycle's path.

But as an American soldier, if you opened fire to defend yourself against what looked like an aggressive motorcycle charge coming at your troops at 40 mph, you had better make damn sure the Taliban was armed. Because if you tried to defend yourself and your troops, and those bodies on the ground after an attempt at self-defense in a war zone are not armed, you had better be ready to face the music with your high command.

By 2012, the same question had grown pervasive throughout American forces in Afghanistan. Would the American chain of command have your back?

Would politically correct rules of engagement, designed to appease the ever-complaining Afghan government of Hamid Karzai, be used to keep Americans from protecting themselves? These questions haunted our troops, and they were questions wrought with life-or-death consequences.

This became the impossible dilemma faced by American ground forces in the 11th year of the Afghan war: defend yourself, and hope like hell that they were armed after you fire; or cross your fingers, and pray that they didn't pull guns and spray you with fire as they passed, toss grenades at you, or blow themselves to hell and back and take you and your buddies with them.

The choice was impossible. But this dilemma had come down from the American high command, which seemed to care more about enforcing politically correct rules of engagement than it cared about the lives of its men.

Even in the weeks before Lieutenant Lorance take over at First Platoon, the Taliban had carried out several high-profile suicide attacks by motorcycle in Afghanistan.

On April 12, 2012, seven American soldiers, members of the Ohio National Guard, had come off the battlefield and retreated into the city of Maimanah, the capital of Farayab Province. They needed respite from the savage war, and visited a park in a more peaceful area of northern Afghanistan.

But in Afghanistan, no place is off limits to the Taliban.

Striking with the surprise of a sudden lightning bolt, their Taliban attacker, mounted on a fast-moving motorcycle, struck out of the blue, a fast-moving human bomb. The explosion killed 10 people, including several of the principal targets, three American soldiers.

Master Sergeant Sgt. Hannon, who died that day, worked for the Department of Veterans Affairs back home as a lawyer serving veterans. With a heart for those who served, including the aging World War II vets, Shawn helped them with their legal needs, putting together wills and health care directives, and giving them advice. Though he could have made tons of money at a private firm, he gave his life to veterans. He was also a great soldier, had been wounded on previous deployment and received the Purple Heart. "If somebody in the world needed help, he'd be there," one of his co-workers told the *Military Times*. Shawn left behind a wife, Jamie, and a son, Evan, who was 9 months old.

Master Sgt. Jeffrey J. Rieck left behind a 15-year-old son, Joel. At a military funeral in Columbus 12 days after the fatal motorcycle attack, Joel accepted the American flag that had been draped on his father's casket from Maj. Gen. Deborah Ashenhurst, the Ohio Guard's commanding officer, who knelt before the boy on one knee.

Capt. Nick Rozanzki, 36, had been married to Jennifer for five years. Their two young daughters are Emma Kathryn and Anna Elizabeth. Nick had been a marathon runner, and an avid soccer player and coach. Volunteering large amounts of time to young people, Nick coached for 15 years for Eagles Soccer Club.

In that one motorcycle attack, two wives lost their husbands, and four children lost their fathers.

The Army calls the weapon that killed these men a "suicide vehicle-borne improvised explosive device." Translated from military-ese to English, it means "motorcycle with a bomb, and impossible to detect before it blows the hell up."

On June 6, 2012, three weeks before Lt. Lorance took over First Platoon, the Taliban carried out another motorcycle attack, this time outside the Kandahar Air Field used by the U.S. Air Force to keep logistics, supplies and reinforcements supplied to the U.S. Army. The suicide motorcyclist charged into a populated area often frequented by American troops.

The massive explosion killed 22 people, and wounded 50. Fortunately, no Americans were in the crowd at the time of the attack, and the "talibiker" killed mostly civilians. But the bloody carnage sent a clear message to all: "If you are an American soldier, or if you work with or near American servicemen, you are a target."

The increase in suicide-bomb-by-motorcycle had sent shock waves throughout U.S. forces in Afghanistan. Against this backdrop, Clint Lorance took command of his platoon on June 29, 2012, determined that none of his boys would be shipped home in body bags. In that noble cause, the lieutenant would succeed.

But it would cost him his freedom.

Chapter 1

U.S. Military Courthouse

Fort Bragg, N.C.

Aug. 1, 2013

1610 Hours (4:10 p.m. EST)

"All rise!"

The military judge, Col. Kirsten V.C. Brunson, U.S. Army, Judge Advocate General's Corps, cloaked in a black robe, stepped into the courtroom and surveyed the scene before her. It had been a long trial, and now, the military jury was about to render its verdict.

Under the soft-white glow of four massive globe lights hanging from the ceiling, the courtroom was packed with a small army of military officers, civilian court personnel, and civilian onlookers. Every face was tense, every eye glued on the judge. The silence, broken only by the solitary cry of the bailiff, was deafening.

Stately dark mahogany desks and barrister rails set against the red burgundy carpet provided a stark contrast to the red-hot tension that now filled the room.

To Judge Brunson's left, when facing the front of the courtroom and the large dark paneled "bench" where the judge is seated, the military jury, or "members" as they are called in the military justice system, had taken their places. Some glanced at the accused. Others looked away, to deliberately avoid eye contact.

"Please be seated."

Col. Brunson was one of the Army's best trial judges. Prior to taking the bench, she had served as the Army JAG Corps' regional defense counsel, managing dozens of junior defense counsel over a large swath of the United States. She had been in this very courtroom many times, but never had the suspense matched this moment. Never had the drama boiled over into the hot anticipation that the next few moments would bring.

Fort Bragg, home of the Army's elite 82nd Airborne Division, the U.S Army Special Operations Command, and the U.S. Army Special Forces Command, was considered its most strategically important military installation. From here,

American Green Berets had launched some of the most important clandestine missions in the nation's history. From here, the famed 82nd Airborne Division had deployed many times in defense of the nation—to Normandy, Market Garden in Holland, the Battle of the Bulge, Vietnam, Grenada, Iraq, and Afghanistan. From Fort Bragg, legendary Delta Force commanders including Col. Charlie Beckwith, Lt. Gen. Jerry Boykin, and Maj. Gen. Bill Garrison had launched clandestine missions all over the world, supporting American interests, from Southeast Asia to Colombia, from Saudi Arabia to Somalia, or any other spot on the globe requiring rapid-response counter-insurgency.

But Fort Bragg was also noted for another, less heroic reason, one the Army would rather blot from the public's memory.

Several of the most publicized military crimes in American history happened on this post. Forty-three years previously, in the most notorious murder case in Fort Bragg history, Green Beret Capt. Jeffrey MacDonald, an Army doctor, was accused of stabbing his wife, Colette, and two young daughters, Kimberly and Kristen, with an ice pick. Their bodies were found in officer housing on Castle Drive. MacDonald had been stabbed, too, in the ribcage, and blamed the crime on drug-crazed hippies. MacDonald's wounds were determined to be self-inflicted, and a federal jury convicted him of triple homicide, of killing his wife and two daughters.

Then came the notorious domestic-murder spree of the summer of 2002, when four Fort Bragg soldiers killed their wives in a period of six weeks. Two were murder-suicides with a gun. A third soldier stabbed his wife 50 times. The fourth strangled his wife to death. These crimes were carried out by some of the Army's most elite, Special Forces soldiers.

Three of the four had just returned from Afghanistan at the time of the murders.

By August of 2013, the memories of these gruesome acts had faded. The MacDonald quarters, preserved many years as a crime scene, was destroyed to make room for a more modern post housing development. Three of the four soldiers from the "Summer of 2002" murder spree were dead. The fourth was imprisoned and incarcerated for his crimes.

Now, all these years later, as Judge Brunson looked out over her courtroom, another soldier in a high-profile case was about to face the verdict of the military justice system. The charges: attempted murder and murder.

First Lt. Clint Lorance, 28 years old, a decorated officer in the elite 82nd Airborne Division, sat at counsel table in his Army service dress blue uniform, moments from his fate. If he felt any fear about what the jury was about to say, his face didn't show it.

While the Lorance case was another in a historical string of high-profile murder prosecutions at Fort Bragg, the facts underlying Clint Lorance's prosecution were different from the others. Very different.

Capt. MacDonald was convicted of stabbing his wife and daughters with an ice pick. The soldiers in the 2002 murder sprees used pistols, knives, and physical strangulation by hand. In contrast, Lt. Clint Lorance never touched a murder weapon, never pulled a trigger, never laid a finger on the men he was accused of killing, and never even saw an alleged victim. Still, the Army had charged him with attempted murder and double murder.

Lorance, the prosecutors claimed, ordered men in his platoon to fire on a motorcycle in a Taliban-invested battle zone in southeastern Afghanistan. At the time of the order, the motorcycle had charged his platoon at a high rate of speed, on a rural dirt road that had been controlled by Taliban forces. Both sides of the road had coiled barbed wire to prevent anyone from entering it.

Signs were placed, in English and Afghan, restricting the roads in the area to only police and military. But coming down a road controlled by the Taliban, the motorcycle kept speeding toward the point where lead elements of the American platoon crossed the road. And, there was not one rider on the motorcycle. There were not two riders on it. But rather, there were three riders on the single red motorcycle.

Lorance knew that the Taliban had used motorcycles as a weapon in suicide missions to blow up Americans in blood-strewn carnages. The prior incidents at Kandahar Airfield and the "talibiker" attack in Farayab Provence provided evidence of the Taliban's suicide-by-motorcycle tactics.

In addition, the month before Lorance arrived, in June of 2012, First Platoon had been battered by the enemy. Four of its 40 men were killed or seriously wounded by land mines, IEDs, or rifle fire. Unidentified and unseen Taliban snipers had fired on the platoon every day. The casualties were so bad, and the landmines so thick, that at the end of June, the Army had pulled First Platoon back off the battlefield for five days for emotional counseling and therapy away from the fighting, and to spend time with "combat stress specialists."

Now, First Platoon had returned to the battlefront, with Lt. Lorance as its new leader. Under the most difficult, dangerous and bloody circumstances imaginable, Clint Lorance's main goal was to keep his men out of body bags, and to keep them from losing limbs and becoming bloody human stumps. American soldiers had suffered enough carnage.

The morning of July 2 promised more burning heat. The searing temperatures, which had eclipsed 100 degrees for 26 out of the last 30 days, had reached 100 degrees by 6 a.m., nearly an hour before they pushed off on their patrol.

After Lt. Lorance conducted his pre-mission briefing around 6:30 a.m., at 6:55 a.m., the platoon left its post on an armed patrol through rows of grape fields and into a Taliban-infested village.

Because the landmines were thick, they were forced to move out from their post in a tight single file, one man behind the other, with mine sweepers out front to detect for lethal bombs in the ground. A step too far to the left or to the right could set off IEDs powerful enough to take out multiple men in a single blast. The plan called for them to move out from their forward operating base, to the west, first through heavily vegetated grape fields, where visibility proved difficult.

They would move through the grape berms for several hundred yards, then turn north, cutting across the grape rows into the small village, known as Sarenzai, where they would move through the back of mud-hut building and then turn and move along the single dirt road through the village. There, they would sweep the village for Taliban operatives, before turning right on the dirt road to head back to their post. Their march pattern resembled a giant fishhook, out into the fields, then looping up into the village, then the spear of the platoon hooking back to the right, down the main road, back toward base.

That was the plan, anyway.

On the route planned for the morning of July 2, the men of First Platoon would cross over much of the same ground that had gotten so many Americans killed or mutilated in recent days. Even after five days of respite and counseling for combat fatigue, that thought loomed at the forefront of their minds as they prepared to return to Taliban country.

Trouble did not procrastinate.

About 10 minutes into their hot patrol, as lead elements of the platoon reached the main road of the village, an emergency call came to Lt. Lorance by radio. Military-aged males with motorcycles were gathering on the far side of the village.

Then, a fast-moving motorcycle appeared. It approached in-bound on the restricted road controlled by the Taliban, closing on their position along the road where his platoon was emerging from the grape fields, and visible to only the Afghans in the lead and the few forward American soldiers.

Lt. Lorance could not see the motorcycle, but one of his paratroopers called out to warn him.

There was no time for debate. No time for introspection or battlefield lawyering. No time to conduct a legal balancing test on whether to use force.

Lorance had to make a split-second decision. Delay could mean death.

Either protect his troops, or cross his fingers and hope that the insurgents on the motorcycle were Santa's helpers from the North Pole, bearing lollypops and candy canes for an early-morning snack for his soldiers as a midsummer's treat. Unable to see the motorcycle himself, his view obstructed by grape berm, and with a split-second of time available to him, in the most Taliban-infested place in the world, Clint ordered his men to open fire. The Afghan National Forces, who were with the American platoon on patrol that morning, also opened fire on the motorcycle.

A shower of bullets rained down on the insurgents, killing two of the three riders. The third rider escaped off into the village, and was never captured.

But when the military found no weapons on the dead riders, Army officials decided to prosecute Clint Lorance for murder, arguing that he had violated the rules of engagement.

It's possible that the bike was strapped with explosives. We will never know. The locals took the bike off the street before the Army could secure it. The Army never recovered the motorcycle.

And now, his court-martial having been completed, First Lt. Lorance would meet his fate.

Inside the new courthouse facility, with Georgian red-brick façade and four towering stark-white columns out front, all eyes were riveted upon the military judge and jury.

Military Judge: "The court is called to order. All parties are again present as before to include the court members. Col. Gabel, has the court reached findings?"

President of the Court Martial (Col. Gabel): "We have, Your Honor."

Military Judge: "And are those reflected on the Findings Worksheet?"

President of the Court Martial (Col. Gabel): "They are, Your Honor."

Military Judge: "Would you please fold that in half and hand it to the bailiff so I can examine it?"

The bailiff retrieved the document from Col. Gabel and handed it to the military judge.

Military Judge: "Please return that to the president."

The bailiff did as directed and returned the document to the president of the court-martial, the military's equivalent to the foreman of the jury.

Military Judge: "The findings appear to be in the proper form. Accused and defense counsel, please rise."

Lorance stood. And as he did, his silver paratroopers' wings, set off against the dark navy blue of his uniform jacket, glistened under the courtroom lights. Below his jump wings were impressive rows of green, orange, red and yellow medals telling the history of his service to his country.

The boyish look on Clint's face contrasted against the erect military bearing that he bore. With four gold buttons lined in a vertical row down the front of his dark-blue jacket, Clint Lorance could have made the cover of an Army recruiting poster. He looked the part, bore the part, and wore the part.

The sharp military appearance was not all that set Lorance apart. For a young officer, who began his career as an enlisted man, Lorance's achievements to date had been spectacular. A quick perusal of his "salad row" showed that he had earned an impressive seven green-and-blue Army Achievement medals, all accumulated in fewer than five years of service.

On top of that, he had been awarded two of the more prestigious dark green-and-white Army Commendation Medals for meritorious service. Perhaps in a dose of unexplainable irony, the most recent Army Commendation Medal had been awarded for the period of time in which Lt. Lorance was charged with attempted murder and double murder.

The medals on his Lorance's chest proclaimed one truth: this officer was a star among his peers. But none of that mattered now. Not if the Army, and not if his country turned on him in this momentous hour.

Military Judge: "Col. Gabel, please announce the findings of the court."

President of the Court Martial: "First Lt. Clint A. Lorance, United States Army, this court-martial finds you—on the charge of attempted murder—guilty. On the charge of double murder—guilty."

http://wbp.bz/toja

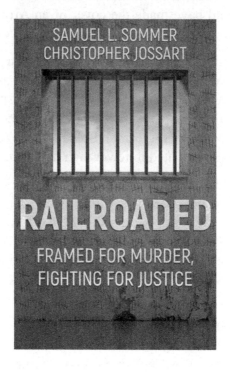
RAILROADED by CHRISTOPHER JOSSART

1.

Stolen in Suffolk

Three men in sharp suits briskly walked toward Sam Sommer's car. Sam looked down at the D on his automatic transmission console inside his Chevy station wagon, grabbed the door handle with his left hand, and poised his right hand atop the horn. His vehicle slowly coasted with one foot on the brake. He wasn't sure whether to squeal out, park and run, lay on the horn, or just keep coasting and jittering.

For someone who made a living making decisions that affected dozens of people each day, Sam couldn't decide what to do in a flash for his own good. His 150-pound furry backseat driver did a better job on demonstrating some damn decisiveness than he did. Sam figured the hell with indecision; it felt better to freeze and hope they would go away. He parked the car—stopping just inside a driveway from a well-travelled street. The unorthodox position of the vehicle appeared foreign to structured rows of parking stalls that filled the lot.

One of the men shouted, "Sommer!" This was all business whomever these good ole' boys were, and the unfolding encounter made Sam realize it included a one-sided agenda. One guy looked familiar from a recent civil, yet macho-style encounter he experienced with a member of Suffolk County law enforcement almost a week ago.

Sam quickly caught a glimpse of an unmarked car parked on the other side of the lot near Walter Court, which runs next to Long Island's busy Jericho Turnpike. The observation of the car parked away from everything else made Sam's already sweaty predicament even more of a salty horror.

He pulled into a Dunkin' Donuts parking lot adjacent to the freeway in Commack, New York, with his big St. Bernard dog. The 2073 Jericho Turnpike establishment opened in 1964 and was a favorite destination for a blossoming community. It was within blocks of Sam's house. The donut shop still stands today near the long-running Mayfair Shopping Center.

Sargent started barking wildly at the sight of oncoming strangers. Sam squinted out the window in an attempt to muster some last-second negotiation to slow the men's collective pace. The way the men marched spelled trouble.

"Who are you and what do you want?" Sam contended. Nothing but steps for an answer, now a few feet from his car.

The pleasant distraction of sweet dough aroma in the air moments earlier was now history. It was replaced with the stench of something dirty going down around 8:10 p.m. on Wednesday, May 22, 1968.

Sargent's momentous fit temporarily distracted the three intruders from their pursuit. The hiccup in an imminent showdown of three-against-one (plus canine) gave Sam an attempt to slide across the seat and exit the passenger side. It was too late for man and best friend. One of the three men had already swung around that side of the car to guard the passenger door.

The man who was shouting "Sommer" identified himself as Detective Thomas Gill with Suffolk County Homicide. The officer, a bit older than Sam, commanded him to join his men in going to the homicide division fourth precinct in nearby Smithtown.

The guy that Sam believed he met days earlier was another detective, Thomas Mansel, who piggybacked Gill's command. "You heard him, Sommer, let's go." Mansel was with the County's Homicide Squad as well.

Sam boldly said he wasn't going anywhere until he learned why.

"Let's go, Sommer," Gill said. He and another man opened the door before Sam could roll up the window and lock his vehicle. They clutched him by the shoulders.

Two men yanked Sam out of his idling station wagon head first in waning daylight at Dunkin' Donuts. Sam thought for a second that the orchestrated grab-and-go was a bad joke somehow tied to a call he received around dinner time to meet someone at the donut shop. He winced in pain from the deep grabs that latched into his sunburned skin. The men rolled Sam to his side on the concrete and cuffed him.

"What the fuck?" cried the thirty-one-year-old family man and business pro in feeble resistance to a kidnapping. Sam's five foot, eight inch frame fell prey to two taller kidnappers. "Stop!" A chorus line of pleas continued during the out-of-the-blue confrontation. While resisting he received a kick in the back of his knee from one of the detectives while being prone on his side for the wide open target. The men quickly dragged Sam across the parking lot toward the unmarked car.

"All right, all right," Sam yelped. Mansel and the other detective following Gill let go of Sam. They lifted him up and let him walk on his own toward their vehicle after a hard shove from Mansel. Sam resumed the journey to the police car voluntarily.

It was still bright enough to notice a man being dragged against his will. Some teenagers had been hanging out in the store for quite some time. Less than a minute before the men left their car from across the lot, Sam entered the Dunkin' Donuts property to meet another man for a meeting concerning one of his business associates, a family relative. The man had not yet arrived, but Sam arrived expecting to wait for him.

Sam slowed his pace toward the car and glanced at the men, expressing concern for Sargent. The dog was left alone in a running car with the driver's side door partially opened. A response came in the form of another shove forward. Sam looked back again toward his station wagon without breaking his stride to catch a glimpse of Sargent. The car bounced like a modern-day pimp mobile from Sargent's display of protection toward his master.

Within feet from the unmarked vehicle, Sam switched his cadence from a defensive tone to one of cooperation. "What's this all about? Please, stop."

Gill opened the back seat door and the other men chucked Sam into the car. After avoiding a brush with his head against the far side door, Sam tried to roll on his back. He was instantly lifted up to a sitting position and buckled. While vehicles zoomed next to one of New York's busiest thoroughfares, a group of men allegedly sworn to serve and protect were stealing a man's freedom amidst the roaring engines.

The door closed to the back seat while Sam realized there were no inside handles. His capturers were in a hurry. The car instantly hit the turnpike and in no time it merged with traffic.

Sam was shaking too much to play eye games with Mansel and Gill, who were seated on each side of him. He just closed his eyes and prayed for the best—whatever that meant. The car quickly exited the turnpike and within a few blocks ended up parked in what seemed like a bumpy lot right next to a main road. That made Sam breathe a little better knowing he wasn't going somewhere far—a self-fulfilling means of fabricating hope.

The driver got out, and Sam asked Gill what this ordeal was about. Gill said he'd find out soon enough and told him to shut up. The driver came back and in less than five minutes the journey to purgatory resumed. No more freeway. Sam arrived in what appeared to be an alley by the narrowing of a street between two lit buildings. He then realized he was at the police station in Hauppauge, a suburb of Smithtown to the south.

It was dusk when the three men placed Sam to his feet in the parking lot of the back entrance to the Suffolk County Fourth Precinct. The whole thing about being around cops suddenly didn't feel right. Sam was supposed to find comfort at a police station; yet, he felt increasingly scared while the three men assertively escorted him toward the back entrance. Once inside, they led Sam down a long hallway to a room on the right.

The average-sized room, about twelve by twelve, was filled with some office equipment, a stool, a couple of chairs, and a square table. It resembled an interrogation room but with a more office-like feel to it. The men immediately shoved Sam against the table and then dropped his fumbling body onto a hard wooden stool and removed his cuffs. They seemed to be setting a tone of play along or it's gonna get physical. The three men convened with a fourth badge from the station outside the room while the door remained open. Sam mulled the connection of a few dots.

How in the world does one go from hooking up with someone in a parking lot to finding a home in a Suffolk County police station in the snap of a finger?

He tried to link learning about the sudden death of his business partner and relative, Irving Silver, to the current madness. Sam flew home last Wednesday, May 15, from Florida by himself while his family remained vacationing with both sets of in-laws. Sam had to deal with a dilemma Silver was having with Sommer's businesses, in particular a man named Harold Goberman.

Goberman was the one who called Sam around dinner time to meet at Dunkin' Donuts regarding Silver's death. Sam recently hired Goberman, who went with an alias of a Harold

Masterson, to do some work at his deli in Commack, the Deli-Queen. His hiring was the result of a recommendation from Silver to help Goberman get reacclimated into society. He retained a vast criminal record and was out of prison on parole. Sam wanted to give the man another chance at life.

Detective Mansel rather forcefully asked Sam to help Suffolk County police identify Silver's body on the afternoon of Friday, May 17. Silver was apparently killed during the early morning on the same day. His body was found on Wheatley Road, a rather unfrequented rural artery off the Jericho Turnpike southeast of Commack.

"You're going to confess, Sommer, right now," instructed Gill in the interrogation room. No identification given of the other men. No reading of any rights concerning a kidnapping called an arrest. The door slammed from the hallway and the same two men who nabbed him plus another stood behind Gill in the crowded room.

"About what?" Sam inquired, still cuffed.

The new man on the scene from the precinct grabbed Sam under his arms and lifted him off of the stool. Gill then pushed Sam head first into the wall and proceeded to shove him onto the floor. Still cuffed, Sam was then harshly seated and punched across the left eye by another officer. His sunburned skin absorbed the beating with needlelike pain.

Another greeting with the concrete floor. Picked up again and placed on the stool, Gill got in Sam's face.

"Want a lawyer, Sommer, or you gonna fess up?"

"For what?" Sam shouted.

"Killing your business buddy," Mansel shouted. "We know you wacked him with a lead pipe and then ran him over. Son of a bitch."

Stunned by what he heard, Sam offered a left-to-right head nod that suggested a nonverbal "No" in reply to the men's accusations. Bewildered with the name Harold Goberman taking over his mind as the centerpiece part of a jigsaw puzzle, Sam started to describe his phone call to Gill tied to a meeting at Dunkin' Donuts.

"A Harold Goberman is behind this" ... stars—a galaxy of pain. A thump on the head by an undetected detective from behind with a telephone book while Sam was held down on the stool blurred his vision. Another whack on the neck from the phone directory ensued in what seemed to be a one-sided conversation. The Goberman mention obviously set off the detectives.

More pounds from the phone book behind Sam's head continued until his ability to sit upright in the stool gave way to the hard floor. Sam laid with his hands over his head and shook enough to trip a Richter scale. His fear couldn't muster any words.

The persuasive techniques used in the basement of Suffolk County's Homicide Unit didn't stop. The men of the badge kicked and yelled at Sam while he curled up on the floor. Realizing there was no other choice but to possibly die, Sam begged to tell the officers about the Goberman phone call. They would have nothing to do with the Goberman thing.

The four men huddled together as if it was fourth-and-goal on the one-yard line and Sam was on defense all by himself. Too pissed off to think about a lawyer, Sam wanted to fight the assholes head on. It was evident there was no more hope for textbook interrogation procedures; it was now all about survival—in a damn police station.

Further beating might have killed Sam. Why didn't they just kill him? That question is still debated today by people who know and love him. God's grace allowed for his story to be told for the benefit of others in the name of justice, Sam offered in retrospect.

"Think about what comes out of your mouth before we come back, Sommer," asserted Gill. The men then left the smoke-filled whipping chamber to the hallway with the door still open. In a cloud of chaos sat a man who a couple of hours earlier left home to learn something to aid in the case of a loved one.

The origination of Sam Sommer's fateful trip to Dunkin' Donuts came with risks and uncertainties in dealing with Goberman. The disgruntled Goberman set Sam up, or so it appeared.

To this day, dear friends Phil and Susan Cirrone from Long Island remember that day more than fifty years later. Philly, as Sam coined the nickname of his close friend, detailed the circumstances leading up to the kidnapping and subsequent aftermath.

A personal recount of horror:

I got a call around 8:00 from Elaine Sommer to come over earlier than planned the evening of the twenty-second of May. We were going to leave shortly anyway to see Elaine's parents visiting from Florida, but Elaine said it was important. We heard earlier in the week that a family member died unexpectedly.

Susan and I are the type of friends to Sammy and Elaine that wouldn't question them in a time of need. We got a babysitter in light of the urgent development and headed to their house.

Upon arrival, Elaine greeted us by the front door. We could tell something was up. She told us that Sam didn't return yet from a meeting at Dunkin' Donuts near the freeway. Elaine didn't have time to go into detail. All she said was that Sam had been involved in trying to find out what happened to her uncle, Irving Silver. She was beside herself; Susan and I were barely inside the door.

Sam was going to meet some guy who had information about Silver at a donut shop. She said Sam drove the station wagon to Dunkin' Donuts with their dog and that something felt wrong.

We didn't know Irving Silver, but Elaine quickly filled us in about his connection to her family and that he was dead. Regardless, friends are friends, and there was no need to pry at the moment about what happened to him. Shocked and saddened by the news, we kept listening. Her parents hugged us and just remained silent the whole time.

Elaine asked me to kindly take her to check on Sammy at Dunkin' Donuts. Of course Susan and I agreed, but first I told Elaine to call the store. She did so and learned Sam wasn't inside the establishment. We then left, determined to find out where he was. Her parents remained at the house for the kids.

The three of us arrived at a nearby Dunkin' Donuts off the turnpike and immediately saw the Sommer's vehicle barely inside the lot from the road. We cautiously circled the car to get a pulse on the situation and noticed their dog going berserk in the back seat.

Creepy shit, yet we remained calm for a horrified Elaine. The lot was well lit and a couple of cars were parked near the store's entrance. Elaine jumped out of our car and yelled to us that Sam's vehicle was still running. We could see, too, that the driver's side door wasn't closed all the way either.

Unquestionably, this was a spine-chilling scene. The dog increased its barking likely from recognizing Elaine. Susan and I both hesitated to go near the car. We advised Elaine not to touch anything and told her that we were going inside the donut shop to see if anyone knew anything. Susan and

I sped to the entrance of the donut shop and ran inside for answers.

Inside the store we couldn't find Sammy, but we found the sight of curiosity all over the joint from the way a couple of workers and a group of kids looked at us. They all appeared dazed.

I was working as a corrections officer at the time and learned a few things when it came to reading people. Susan kept an eye on Elaine while I asked the manager what was going on. Sweat drenched my shirt. Where in the hell was Sammy?

A few teenagers congregated around the counter in front of the manager. He said the person in the car who parked weirdly in his lot was taken by some guys. One of the teens chimed in and said the man he thinks we were talking about was dragged out of his car and taken away (pointing in the direction of the turnpike). Another teen described the dog in the back seat running around so wildly that the car bounced.

Susan and I grabbed hold of one another. "What?" we collectively bellowed. "Like kidnapped?" I piggybacked the disbelief with a question to continue the inquisition. We froze with jaws on the floor. The first kid said they were like gangsters and asked if we knew the guy who was taken.

The store manager indicated that the men, unable to recall how many for sure—a few he proclaimed, looked like a bunch of wise guys. Another teen said that they looked like bad asses and one of them carried a gun. The same youngster believed there were three men working together against one victim.

I asked the manager if he called the cops. He said no. I got the impression he wanted to look the other way, so to speak. The kids were kind enough to wish us well and they split, too, likely not wanting to stick around much longer. The described mobster-type men had everyone on edge.

On the verge of calling the police, I noticed a cop car pull into the lot. It felt comforting, yet odd. If no one called the police how would they know what was going on? Maybe someone else around the neighborhood or store called, I thought. Anyway, Susan went outside toward Elaine, who quickly grabbed the officer's attention for obvious reasons. I made a quick call to a lawyer friend of mine to explain what was going down and then joined the commotion outside.

The front driver's side door was part way open. A slimy mist, like dew, covered most of the windows, probably from the dog's cries. It didn't look like Sammy was around. All eyes fixated on the cop for answers. Car running. Dog freaking out. No Sammy. The officer then did a quick search of the car.

Elaine then left with the officer to go across the way a short distance to the Mayfair Shopping Center to use a phone. We just stood by the car trying to comfort the dog without being able to touch anything. The biggest thing we couldn't touch was reality. We were scared and more so for Sammy.

The officer said that he and Elaine would be back in a matter of minutes. Their poor dog's barks grew hoarser. I told Susan that I called Joe Scibilia, and that he might be able to help Sammy from a legal standpoint, if needed.

Like the officer promised, he returned with Elaine. She looked as mad as she did worried a few moments ago. I asked what was going on. The officer informed us that he called the station to see if there was anything on Mr. Sommer. I could tell Elaine was pissed. She then insisted that her husband was kidnapped. Just hearing that word sent shivers through my body.

The officer said that she would need to fill out a Missing Persons Report at the police station in Hauppauge. He told Elaine that she could take the car home (for perceived concern about the dog). The cop's intention appeared heartfelt toward the dog; yet, I found it strange that he would release the car back to its owner so quickly. Theoretically, this location and the vehicle itself could still be considered a potential crime scene, I thought.

Here's what else seemed screwed up. The officer didn't write anything down up until this point. From my years in corrections, documentation means everything. Writing something down gave an impression of importance and focus. How do you dismiss a running car with the driver's side door left open and a dog going nuts in the back seat as anything not related to foul play?

Nonchalantly like another day at the office, the officer reminded us of the Missing Persons Report and departed the scene. His calmness drove me nuts. No urgency. It was going to be a long night.

Susan skillfully excelled in the field of empathy. She was a gentle offset to my dealing with hard asses all the time. I thanked her for comforting Elaine. I trusted her more than myself to handle Elaine the best way possible given the circumstance. I was too upset at this farce of an investigation.

We both agreed to bring the vehicle and dog back to Sam's home. It might buffer the heart-stopping news a bit for Elaine about her husband, and frankly, the dog was pretty messed up. Susan and I followed Elaine back to her house where she parked the car and took the dog inside. A neighbor was watching the Sommer kids, and the three of us proceeded to the fourth precinct.

Susan guided a tear-drenched Elaine into the back seat of our car, and in a flash we took off to get this report done. Maybe then we could start to get somewhere concerning Sammy. There we went... into the waning abyss of hell known as May 22, 1968.

***

Gill and his men quickly returned to Sam's abuse chamber from just outside the room at the Suffolk County Fourth Precinct Homicide Division. A day etched in lawlessness against a hardworking young man, husband, and father of seven came close to an end—at least based on the time of day. Sam didn't know if these sworn men of honor were just getting warmed up for an all-nighter or maybe an amateur form of execution.

Sitting with his head resting on a small table, Sam fielded a command from Gill to get up and pay attention. He gingerly rose and hunched over in a state of pain and stood as attentive as possible. A slap to the back of Sam's head and neck with a phone book now serving as a weapon staggered him from wall-to-wall in another round of late night captivity. He felt like dying. Gill felt impatient, like he didn't want to be there and would rather have the whole thing over with.

Lowered back in the chair, Sam's head tilted toward God in prayer of something to happen—heaven or home. Surrounded by folded arms and smoky drags around the table, Gill leaned into his helpless prey. "Fess up, Sommer."

The verbal onslaughts that previously followed with a physical bashing took a different turn this time. Two men behind Sam rather gently lifted him upright. What should have felt comforting seemed creepy to Sam. After he was lifted, the stool beneath him was removed and the detectives laid him on the ground. The men ripped his t-shirt and removed his clothes. Sam curled into a ball on a cold floor, stark naked.

"Gonna speak now, Sommer," one of the detectives asked pompously in a new twist of torture. The room succumbed to silence. Suffolk County's interrogation techniques were building in stunning infamy. "Come on, Sommer," insisted Gill or Mansel based on Sam's aged recollection. "Fess up."

"Florida," Sam uttered from his shell. No response. No punches. No accusations. He prayed for even a belch in the room. The stillness defined a level of fear that Sam never fathomed. He believed the next phase in this scheme was death. He knew that protecting himself was even more of a fairy tale since he wasn't wearing any clothes.

Sam lifted his head a smidgeon to see that the men walked away from the table. In the first act of a humane tone since getting seized from a donut shop parking lot, Gill calmly inquired, "Tell us more, Sommer, about Florida. What the hell does that mean?"

Sam as a suspect suddenly had a voice in this assumed interrogation proceeding going down in the final hours of May 22. The interrogators welcomed his voice for the first time outside the realm of being toyed with to make a false confession. "Took my family to Florida... came back early to help Silver deal with a matter about the business," murmured a drained Sam.

"You told me last week you were going to meet Silver, and that was around the time he was wacked," Mansel reminded Sam.

"We were working together on some bad shit with Goberman—you need to talk to Harold Goberman," uttered the helpless suspect.

No reply. Sam heard some shuffling of feet and a whisper or two. He could sense growing frustration in the room among the badges. He predicted that these guys weren't going to leave him alone until they got what they sought—a confession to the murder of Irving Silver. His prediction materialized. In so many testy words, Gill told him that he needed to give them what they wanted so they could wrap up the investigation.

At one point the detectives moved Sam into a basement room for a few minutes. His state of confusion disallowed him to really make heads or tails of what was going on. Since Sam was so weak, he kind of went with the flow during this peculiar little tour of the precinct's lower level. The detectives didn't say much—it seemed like they were hiding him. Within moments, they returned Sam upstairs to his original interrogation room.

The smell of judicial corruption took over. Whoever was orchestrating the targeting of Sam Sommer was friends with the devil. 'What the…?' Sam internalized while wincing in pain moving his exposed body to the floor. 'This is serious shit. First, a dead relative. Then a phone call from a guy we were trying to help get his life together, followed by getting nabbed from my own damn car to having the shit kicked out of me and stripped. Why ask me about Florida and then disregard it?'

***

Phil Cirrone and the two ladies arrived at the same Suffolk County precinct near Smithtown where Sam was getting tortured. Unaware of that coincidence upon arrival, Philly tried to work over the officers by way of influence as a member of the New York City Department of Corrections. He started to flex his relational muscle for the Sommers to get some real answers.

Bingo, but not on Philly's card. No more than a couple of minutes after the three entered the station, Susan recognized a friend of her brother, an FBI special agent. He was there conducting some business related to a case on Long Island.

"Remember me?" asked Susan. "I'm Marvin's sister."

"Yes," replied the agent. "You're"…

"Susan, Susan Cirrone."

She briefly small talked about her brother after shaking hands with the agent. She then reintroduced her husband, recalling their paths crossed before through her brother. Phil was consumed in watching over Elaine so Susan could converse with her brother's friend. Elaine wanted to speak to someone in charge, ASAP.

"What brings you here? Is everything OK?" the agent asked Susan.

Phil introduced Elaine to the agent, and she explained the situation to him with reference to Sam's name. Expecting support related to the process of reporting a missing person, the three instead hear an Orson Wells-caliber revelation.

"I think he's down the hall, locked up."

Paled and going through her own version of abuse from yet another bomb dropped, Elaine darted toward a long hallway, the direction in which the agent glanced when he made the claim. Phil grabbed Elaine's arm and slowed her enough to allow Susan to thank the agent and apologize for the trouble. The three citizen investigators of Sam heard the word "locked," and an aura of injustice dismissed the conversation.

The agent embarrassingly gathered that he shouldn't have disclosed Sam's whereabouts. He added out of desperation to deflect the situation elsewhere, "They've moved him to another precinct. It's common to rotate someone... uh." The agent stopped talking and left abruptly.

Whether he was lying or inferred "elsewhere" as being a hospital remains unsettled today. The agent could not later testify to such a claim for obvious reasons of conflict of interest. Incidentally, Sam was moved from his first-floor interrogation room to a similar room in the basement at some point between 10:00 and 11:00 that night. He believes to this day the move was made out of fear by the police that three people were there looking for him.

After the agent split, Phil's gut told him that Sam was still down the hall. He led the ladies past the front desk on a mission. *Authorized Personnel Only* signs warned of their against-the-grain gamble to another part of the building. One officer emerged from another room past the desk and thwarted their journey. He sandwiched the Sam-seekers. Right out of a movie.

Elaine was in no mood to be trapped by the very people who may have something to do with her husband's quandary. The officers instructed the organic search party to leave the unauthorized location. Elaine wasn't accepting such orders. She demanded to know where her husband was.

The front desk officer said he would make a call for her. After a few attempts, the officer verified that her husband was taken into custody. He told her that he was relocated to another part of the multiple-facility complex. This was a far cry difference than what she heard a few minutes earlier that there was no Sam Sommer on site for sake of interviewing or lodging. The officer insisted that Elaine go home and that her husband would call her.

A salty and red-faced Elaine Sommer slowly made her way out of the station under the care of Phil and Susan. She wondered where Sam was—the rock in her world, loving husband, lover of the Lord Jesus Christ, and devoted father who'd been building American Dreams for so many people. Elaine felt empty without the strength to take another step toward the Cirrone's car. Sam wouldn't be coming home tonight was all her mind held.

It was late. Wednesday, May 22, 1968, was winding down into a day of sobering consequences to whatever Suffolk County, New York wants, it supposedly gets.

Sam did not confess to killing Irving Silver from his holding cell or anytime afterward. On a note pad, Sam recalled Thomas Gill recording that he did confess. The "official" form of documentation resembled a third-grader pulling out a piece of paper from his desk to draw a picture at will.

Finally, the brutality ended. The detectives escorted Sam across a parking lot to a different building where he was photographed, fingerprinted, and processed for arrest and lodging purposes. They then transported him to a hospital in Riverhead, New York, to be treated for injuries. He then slept a few winks in a cell at the Suffolk County Riverhead Police Station.

http://wbp.bz/railroadeda

See even more at:
http://wbp.bz/tc

More True Crime You'll Love From WildBlue Press

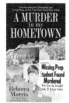

A MURDER IN MY HOMETOWN by Rebecca Morris

Nearly 50 years after the murder of seventeen year old Dick Kitchel, Rebecca Morris returned to her hometown to write about how the murder changed a town, a school, and the lives of his friends.

wbp.bz/hometowna

THE BEAST I LOVED by Robert Davidson

Robert Davidson again demonstrates that he is a master of psychological horror in this riveting and hypnotic story ... I was so enthralled that I finished the book in a single sitting. "—James Byron Huggins, International Bestselling Author of The Reckoning

wbp.bz/tbila

BULLIED TO DEATH by Judith A. Yates

On September 5, 2015, in a public park in LaVergne, Tennessee, fourteen-year-old Sherokee Harriman drove a kitchen knife into her stomach as other teens watched in horror. Despite attempts to save her, the girl died, and the coroner ruled it a "suicide." But was it? Or was it a crime perpetuated by other teens who had bullied her?

wbp.bz/btda

SUMMARY EXECUTION by Michael Withey

"An incredible true story that reads like an international crime thriller peopled with assassins, political activists, shady FBI informants, murdered witnesses, a tenacious attorney, and a murderous foreign dictator."—Steve Jackson, New York Times bestselling author of NO STONE UNTURNED

wbp.bz/sea

Made in the USA
Coppell, TX
13 April 2020

19750988R00148